A BENN STUDY . DRAMA

THE NEW MERMAIDS

Three Late Medieval Morality Plays

Three Late Medieval Morality Plays

MANKIND EVERYMAN
MUNDUS ET INFANS

Edited by

G. A. LESTER

*Lecturer in English Language,
University of Sheffield*

LONDON/ERNEST BENN LIMITED

NEW YORK/W. W. NORTON AND COMPANY INC.

First published in this form 1981
by Ernest Benn Limited
25 New Street Square, Fleet Street, London EC4A 3JA
& Sovereign Way, Tonbridge, Kent TN9 1RW

© *Ernest Benn Limited 1981*

Published in the United States of America by
W. W. Norton and Company Inc.
500 Fifth Avenue, New York, N.Y. 10036

Distributed in Canada by
The General Publishing Company Limited, Toronto
Printed in Great Britain by
Fakenham Press Limited, Fakenham, Norfolk.

British Library Cataloguing in Publication Data

Three late medieval moralities.—(The New
   mermaids)
   1. English drama—to 1500
   2. English drama—Early modern and Elizabethan,
   1500–1600
   I. Lester, Godfrey Allen   II. Series
   822'.2   PR1262

ISBN 0–510–33505–5

CONTENTS

ACKNOWLEDGEMENTS

IN PREPARING THIS EDITION I have benefited from the accumulated wisdom of several generations of editors and critics. The sensible unmodernized editions of *Mankind* by Mark Eccles and *Everyman* by A. C. Cawley have been especially useful, and so too has the facsimile and transcription of *Mankind* by D. M. Bevington, which lightened the burden of working from the sometimes barely legible manuscript. Smart's extensive notes on *Mankind*, and the standard collections of traditional sayings by Tilley, Whiting, and in *The Oxford Dictionary of English Proverbs* have also been helpful, and my starting point was, as for all students of pre-Shakespearian drama, Carl J. Stratman's *Bibliography of Medieval Drama* (New York, 1972). I have received much valued advice from a number of colleagues and friends, especially Professor Norman Blake, Dr John Widdowson, Mrs Johanna Hunter, Mr Brian Donaghey, Dr J. Stangroom, Mrs N. Hodges, and from Miss Roma Gill, general editor of this series. I wish also to thank Mrs Sandra Burton for cheerfully and efficiently typing my manuscript; Poculi Ludique Societas of Toronto for bringing *Mankind* and *Mundus et Infans* to life in two excellent performances in Dublin in 1980, which helped clear up several practical difficulties; and finally my family, who went without a proper holiday so that I might have time to put the edition together.

Figures 1 and 2 are reproduced by kind permission of the Trustees of the British Library; figures 3 and 4 by kind permission of the Board of Trinity College, Dublin.

Sheffield   G.A.L.
December 1980

ABBREVIATIONS

1. *Texts of Plays*

MS	Washington D.C., Folger MS V.a.354, ff.122–34r
A	*Everyman*, printed by John Skot, *c.* 1528–29 [*STC* 10606]
B	*Everyman*, printed by John Skot, *c.* 1530–35 [*STC* 10605]
C	*Everyman*, printed by Richard Pynson, *c.* 1510–25 [*STC* 10604]
D	*Everyman*, printed by Richard Pynson, *c.* 1525–30 [*STC* 10603]
Q	*Mundus et Infans*, printed by Wynkyn de Worde, 1522 [*STC* 25982]
Bevington	D. M. Bevington (ed), *Medieval Drama* (Boston, 1975)
Cawley	A. C. Cawley (ed), *Everyman* (Manchester, 1961)
Eccles	M. Eccles (ed), *The Macro Plays* (London, EETS O.S.262, 1969)
Hick Scorner	*Hick Scorner* in I. Lancashire (ed), *Two Tudor Interludes* (Manchester, 1980)
Jack Juggler	*Jack Juggler* in J. S. Farmer (ed), *Anonymous Plays, Third Series* (London, 1906)
Magnificence	*Magnificence: John Skelton*, ed P. Neuss (Manchester, 1980)
Manly	J. M. Manly (ed), *Specimens of the Pre-Shakesperian-Drama* (Boston, 1897)
Nature	*Nature* in J. S. Farmer (ed), *'Lost' Tudor Plays* (London, 1907)
Perseverance	*The Castle of Perseverance* in Eccles
Pride of Life	*The Pride of Life* in P. Happé (ed), *Tudor Interludes* (Harmondsworth, 1972)
Youth	*The Interlude of Youth* in I. Lancashire (ed), *Two Tudor Interludes*

2. *Other Works*

AV	Authorized Version of the Bible
Canterbury Tales	*The Canterbury Tales* in *The Works of*

vii

	Geoffrey Chaucer, ed F. N. Robinson (London, 1957)
Confessio Amantis	*Confessio Amantis* in *The Complete Works of John Gower* ed G. C. Macaulay (Oxford, 1901)
Craik	T. W. Craik, *The Tudor Interlude* (Leicester, 1958)
EETS	Early English Text Society
Jacob's Well	*Jacob's Well,* ed A. Brandeis (London, EETS O.S. 115, 1900)
Lancashire	I. Lancashire, "The Auspices of *The World and the Child*", *Renaissance and Reformation* 12 (1976), 96–105
Lay Folks' Catechism	*The Lay Folks' Catechism,* ed T. F. Simmons and H. E. Nolloth (London, EETS O.S. 118, 1901)
Materialien	*Materialien zur Kunde des älteren Englischen Dramas*
MED	*Middle English Dictionary,* ed H. Kurath and S. M. Kuhn (Ann Arbor, 1952–)
OED	*The Oxford English Dictionary*
Oxford Proverbs	*The Oxford Dictionary of English Proverbs* (Oxford, 1970)
Smart	W. K. Smart, 'Some Notes on *Mankind*', *MP* 14 (1916), 45–58, 293–313
STC	A. W. Pollard and G. R. Redgrave, *A Short-Title Catalogue of Books Printed in England, Scotland, and Ireland and of English Books Printed Abroad, 1475–1640* (London, 1926)
Sugden	E. H. Sugden, *A Topographical Dictionary to the Works of Shakespeare and his Fellow Dramatists* (Manchester, 1925)
Tilley	M. P. Tilley, *A Dictionary of the Proverbs in England in the Sixteenth and Seventeenth Centuries* (Ann Arbor, 1950)
Whiting	B. J. Whiting, *Proverbs, Sentences, and Proverbial Phrases from English Writings mainly before 1500* (Cambridge, Mass., and London, 1968)

3. *Journals*

AHR	*American Historical Review*
HSN	*Harvard Studies and Notes in Philology and Literature*

JEGP	*Journal of English and Germanic Philology*
MLN	*Modern Language Notes*
MP	*Modern Philology*
MS	*Mediaeval Studies*
N&Q	*Notes and Queries*
PMLA	*Publications of the Modern Language Association of America*
PQ	*Philological Quarterly*
SP	*Studies in Philology*

4. *Other Abbreviations*

ed.	this edition
E.S.	Extra Series
N.S.	New Series
O.S.	Original Series
r.w.	rhyming with
s.d.	stage direction
s.p.	speech prefix

Biblical quotations in Latin are from the Vulgate text in *Biblia Sacra Juxta Vulgatam Clementinam* (Rome etc, 1956); those in English are from the Douay-Rheims. Douay-Rheims is a very literal translation of the Vulgate, and is therefore used here in preference to the more familiar Authorized Version[AV], which in places is quite different. In references to the Psalms in which the Vulgate numbering differs from that of AV, the AV numbering is also given. Mystery Plays are cited from Bevington, unless indicated otherwise.

INTRODUCTION

MORALITY PLAYS

THE MORALITY PLAY, which was popular in England between about 1400 and about 1600, has been defined as 'the dramatization of a spiritual crisis in the life of a representative mankind figure in which his spiritual struggle is portrayed as a conflict between personified abstractions representing good and evil'.[1] This rule-of-thumb definition is a useful starting point, but, like all genre definitions, it falls short of the whole truth. Certainly, many of the characters are 'personified abstractions' (such as Beauty, Conscience); but others are generalized types (Fellowship, Cousin); while others act *in propria persona* (God, the Devil);[2] and the protagonist is not so much a representative of all mankind as a representative Christian. So it is unwise to attempt to define too narrowly a term which was, in any case, not in use in the fifteenth and sixteenth centuries, for contemporaries called these plays not 'Morality Plays' but 'Moral Plays' or simply 'Interludes'. Of the three plays here presented, *Mankind* is untitled, *Mundus et Infans* is twice called an Interlude, and the title page of *Everyman* announces 'a treatise . . . in manner of a moral play', the same term as is used by the Messenger who acts as prologue:

I pray you all give your audience
And hear this matter with reverence,
By figure a moral play!

Emphasis on the plays' moral lesson and the general tendency to make unfavourable comparisons with the plays of Shakespeare and other humanist playwrights have understandably undermined their appeal, yet many volumes of modern criticism have proclaimed Shakespeare's indebtedness to the morality tradition,[3] and an increasing number of modern revivals is all the time demonstrating their theatrical effectiveness. Morality plays are now counted as tried examples of living theatre, and have even been

[1] Bevington, p. 792.
[2] See W. R. Mackenzie, *The English Moralities from the Point of View of Allegory* (Boston and London, 1914), pp. 5–8.
[3] Three of the most important are B. Spivack, *Shakespeare and the Allegory of Evil* (New York and London, 1958); D. M. Bevington, *From 'Mankind' to Marlowe* (Cambridge, Mass., 1962); G. Wickham, *Shakespeare's Dramatic Heritage* (London, 1969).

shown susceptible of transition to a modern idiom.[4] There can be few plays as daringly racy as *Mankind*, as wildly disrespectful, as resourceful in involving the audience, and yet as committed to a serious and consistent moral end. Few could equal *Everyman* for its sombre and disquieting treatment of the uncomfortably inevitable condition, death. Even *Mundus et Infans,* while not of the same consistently high quality as the others, interestingly adapts common medieval themes like transience, vainglory, and the ages of man's life (well known from the famous speech of melancholy Jaques) to preach the same message: that every man must sin, but that even the most wicked is not beyond hope.

Surviving plays which are thought of as Moralities, or of Morality type, number about sixty,[5] and the three in this edition are among the first ten. The others are *The Pride of Life* (c.1400), now only a fragment, in which the King of Life arrogantly challenges Death to a duel; *The Castle of Perseverance* (1400–25), the most magnificent of the moralities, 3,650 lines long with a character list of 36, which traces the life of Humanum Genus (i.e. Mankind) from birth to death and beyond; *Wisdom* (c. 1460), an elaborate demonstration of the waywardness of the three powers of the soul, Mind, Will, and Understanding; *Nature* (c. 1495), by Henry Medwall, which dramatizes the fall, recovery, and second lapse of Man, before he finally turns to Reason in his old age; *Hick Scorner* and the closely related *Youth* (both c. 1514), which show the susceptibility of young people to contemporary social and moral evils; and *Magnificence* (c. 1520) by John Skelton, a 'Mirror for Princes' containing much contemporary social satire, including in the character Magnificence a thinly-veiled allusion to Cardinal Wolsey.

AUTHORS

Mankind, like the other plays in this volume, is anonymous, but a few suppositions may nonetheless be made concerning the author. The places named in the play are mostly villages near Cambridge and King's Lynn, East Anglian towns some forty miles apart, and there are some slight signs that the author's knowledge of the former locality was the more thorough.[6] He knew Latin well, and had some knowledge of the law; he had a sound grasp of theology, but, like many medieval writers, was critical of the established

---

[4] See Wickham, op. cit., pp. 32–3.

[5] For a convenient list, with plot summaries and bibliographies, see P. J. Houle, *The English Morality and Related Drama* (Hamden, Conn., 1972).

[6] Smart, pp. 306–9.

church; he was, in the context of this play at least, more interested in the broad issues of sin and forgiveness than in the specific ecclesiastical institutions related to these (contrast the easy forgiveness of the repentant Mankind with the detailed course of contrition, confession, absolution, and satisfaction which is prescribed for Everyman); his informed interest in both Latin and vernacular rhetoric, coupled with his delight in verbal parody, suggests that he may have been connected with the university of Cambridge;[7] and above all his 'theatrical' flair points to the possibility that he was a professional or experienced amateur actor himself.

There is nothing in *Everyman* to help identify the author, other than the evidence that he knew some Dutch, for *Everyman* is almost certainly a translation of the Dutch play *Elckerlijc*. A man who is known to have translated several books from Dutch for the English market is one Laurence Andrewe of Calais, who worked as a printer and bookseller in London in and after 1527;[8] but, in the absence of firm evidence, any connection between Andrewe and *Everyman* is pure conjecture.

Mundus et Infans is based on a late fourteenth- or early fifteenth-century poem on the ages of man, to which one of the most imaginative changes has been the compression of a whole range of evils into the one Vice, Folly. It may be significant, then, that the only specific local allusions are in Folly's speeches, and these are all to places in London—Holborn, Westminster, Eastcheap, The Inns of Court, Newgate, London Bridge and The Pope's Head Tavern. For the dubious practices with which these places are associated the dramatist seems to draw on a genuine knowledge of local reputations, and on these grounds it seems likely that he was an inhabitant of London.[9]

DATES

Mankind survives in a manuscript of the second half of the fifteenth century. The date of composition of the play can be narrowed down with the help of several pieces of internal evidence. Amongst

---

[7] See the discussion of the audience of *Mankind*, p. xxxvi.

[8] Cawley, p. xiii.

[9] *Mundus et Infans* 571–3, 585, 591, 671–3, 791 and notes. Lancashire, p. 100, suggests that the play was written for a provincial gentleman, and cites Folly's remark (line 669) as evidence that the original place of production was a day's ride from London. He suggests the sponsor may have been Richard, earl of Kent (d. 1523).

the most useful are the many references to current money, including one to the *royal* (line 465), a gold coin which was first issued in 1464–65.[10] The name had not been in use for any earlier coin, so an earlier date than 1464 is out of the question, and one would expect a time-lag of several years before the new coins became so generally known as to be mentioned in the play. Moreover, there are allusions to every piece of current coin in use in England in the second half of the fifteenth century with the sole exception of the *angel*, which made its appearance between 1468 and 1470. While it is dangerous to argue from negative evidence, the absence of reference could suggest that the *angel*, which became a popular coin, was not known at the time, in which case a date in the very early 1470s would be the *terminus at quem*. Another piece of evidence is an uncomplimentary reference to an imaginary 'Pope Pocket' (lines 143–4),[11] possibly merely a generalized jibe at papal avarice (to the apparently bottomless 'pocket' of the papacy), but possibly also a reference to John Poket, who from 1444 to 1464 was prior of Barnwell Abbey, near Cambridge, the region in which *Mankind* is believed to have originated. The allusion is the more likely since Prior Poket is known to have had dealings with 'Master Allington of Bottisham' (line 514), and to have been a papal representative in the area, which would explain the ironic title 'Pope'. Prior Poket died in 1464, but his reputation in the area could have survived him by a number of years. There is also the apparently disrespectful reference to 'King Edward the Nought . . . in the regnal year of no king' (though this occurs in a passage of deliberately garbled Latin, lines 686–92, the meaning of which is not beyond dispute).[12] The remark might point to the period between October 1470, when Edward IV fled the country, and May 1471, when he regained the throne. The 'Master Allington' of line 514 was in exile with Edward, but this temporary absence need not imply that the play could not have been written then. Altogether, 1464–71 is as precise a date as one can safely assume.

The other two plays are first found in print. The earliest of the *Everyman* editions is the fragment C, printed by Richard Pynson between *c.* 1510 and 1525.[13] However, Greg has shown, from bibliographical evidence, that there was a textual history which may take the composition of *Everyman* back some time before the Pynson print.[14] Moreover, Van Mierlo has argued that the English

[10] See D. C. Baker, 'The Date of *Mankind*', *PQ* 42 (1963), 90–1.

[11] See T. J. Jambeck and R. R. Lee, '"Pope Pokett" and the date of *Mankind*', *MS* 39 (1977), 511–13.

[12] See Smart, p. 45; Eccles, p. xxxviii.

[13] See the Note on the Text.

[14] *Materialien* 28 (Louvain, 1910), pp. 60–9. See also Cawley, p. x.

version is based on Vorsterman's Antwerp print of *Elckerlijc* (*c.* 1518–25); if he is correct, a date of *c.* 1520 for the English play seems likely, though a late fifteenth-century date is often suggested.[15]

The unique early print of *Mundus et Infans* has a colophon which at first sight seems to provide conclusive evidence of date:

> Here endeth the Interlude of Mundus et Infans, Imprinted at London in Fleet Street at the Sign of the Sun by me, Wynkyn de Worde, the Year of our Lord MCCCCC and xxii, the xvii day of July.

However, the interlude was probably not entirely 'new' in 1522, despite the claim to this effect on de Worde's title-page, for the day-book of John Dorne, an Oxford bookseller, records under the year 1520 the sale of 'mundus a play' at a price of two pence.[16] The play itself also shows its age. One does not have to be a philologist to spot the many deficiencies of style, sense, and language, ranging from the missing lines which disrupt the stanza patterns to deficiencies of sense and spoiled rhymes.[17] These features suggest that the play circulated for some time in manuscript before reaching print, and that the errors which had accumulated were un-critically accepted in the printed edition. A date of composition some time before 1520 therefore seems likely.

SOURCES AND ANALOGUES

Morality Plays have been traced to a variety of supposed sources, none of which by itself could have been the origin of the genre, although all have no doubt had their influence. One is the fourth-century poem *Psychomachia* ('The War of the Soul') by Prudentius, in which vices engage virtues in a series of combats.[18] A struggle

---

[15] J. Van Mierlo, *Elckerlijc: Nieuwe Bijdragen met Ge-emendeerde Uitgave* (Turnhout, 1949), pp. 22–31. Lancashire, *Two Tudor Interludes*, pp. 38–9, argues that the Interlude of *Youth* is in places influenced by *Everyman*. This would place Everyman before *c.* 1514, the probable date for the composition of *Youth*. But the verbal and thematic parallels are nowhere so close as to establish a certain connection between the two plays.

[16] See C. R. L. Fletcher (ed), *Collectanea* I (Oxford, Oxford Historical Society, 1885), p. 130; also H. N. MacCracken, 'A Source of *Mundus et Infans*', *PMLA* 23 (1908), 486.

[17] Missing lines and irregular stanzas are detailed in the Note on the Text. For a deficiency of sense which is unlikely to be a mere printing error see line 929n. Examples of spoiled rhymes are self-evident, even when allowance is made for the fact that the dramatist seems in places to have been satisfied with the faintest degree of assonance in lieu of rhyme. MacCracken, ibid., 486n, suggests a late fifteenth-century date; Craik, supported by Lancashire, suggests 1508?

[18] See Spivack, op. cit., pp. 60–95.

between good and evil for the possession of the soul is certainly basic to all Morality Plays, and even takes the form of a pitched battle in *The Castle of Perseverance,* which is more dependent than any other on the *Psychomachia.* But to envisage man's soul as merely the prize of war is to deny man the power to influence his own fate, and, since the plays strongly emphasize that man has the free will to choose the right way or to reject it, the *Psychomachia*'s importance should not be overstressed. Along the same lines is the suggestion that the Moralities developed from the Paternoster Plays,[19] civic dramas of which no example survives, but which are known from records to have been performed at York, Beverley, and Lincoln from the fourteenth century to the sixteenth. It seems that the plays were based on the doctrine that within the Lord's Prayer lie the seven 'remedies' to the seven deadly sins. With this as the thematic basis 'all manner of vices and sins were held up to scorn, and the virtues were held up to praise'. These plays, nearer to the Moralities in time, place, and genre, surely had a formative influence, but in the absence of more evidence it would be unwise to stress their importance too much. A third idea is that the Morality Plays are a dramatic development of the sermon.[20] Medieval preachers, particularly the friars, were constantly on the look-out for means to bring their sermons to life and drive their message home. One of the ways was to enliven the sermon with *exempla*, figures and narratives calculated both to capture the interest of the listeners and to give intelligible proportions to the moral point. (Chaucer's *Pardoner's Tale* is a good example.) In both *Everyman* and *Mundus et Infans* the protagonists offer themselves as *exempla* when they say to the audience:

Take example, all ye that this do hear or see ...   (*Everyman* 867)

and

Now sirs, take all ensample by me ...   (*Mundus et Infans* 961)

Some of the plots of the Moralities can be traced to sermon *exempla*; so, too, can much of the moral and theological exposition; and most Moralities contain addresses to the audience which are really mini-sermons in their own right. But the better plays teach through action as well as words, and the sermons have little to tell of how this might have come about. So we would be wise to regard the Moralities as products of a complex web of influences of which the *Psychomachia*, Paternoster Plays, and sermons are three of the most important. To these should be added the Mystery Plays and other

[19] Bevington, pp. 792–3.
[20] Cawley, pp. xiii–xiv. See also P. Neuss, 'Active and Idle Language; Dramatic Images in *Mankind*' in *Medieval Drama*, ed N. Denny (London, 1973), pp. 41–4.

vernacular dramas, debate poems such as that between the soul and the body, works exemplifying the seven deadly sins and their various sub-divisions, the religious lyrics treating of the brevity of life, of the horrors of death, and of the efficacy of the Passion; and not least the countless works, including *The Romance of the Rose* and *Piers Plowman*, which popularized the allegorical mode and familiarized the use of personification.[21]

Mankind has been likened to parts of the poem *The Assembly of Gods*, to parts of *Piers Plowman*, to the anonymous dialogue *Mercy passeth Righteousness*, and to a sermon on mercy in the fifteenth-century homilists' manual *Jacob's Well*;[22] but these are, at most, influences not sources. In fact, doctrine and dramatic action are so skilfully blended in *Mankind* that the author's use of any single, specific, non-dramatic source is extremely unlikely.

In contrast, *Everyman*'s immediate source is now fairly certainly established as the late fifteenth-century Flemish Morality *Elckerlijc*. Much labour has been devoted to deciding the issue of priority, for it has proved difficult for scholars to accept that so fine a play as *Everyman* could be the work of a man who (it is argued) failed at times to present Biblical material correctly,[23] introduced errors of logic,[24] and misunderstood the rhyme scheme[25] and even the literal meaning of his original.[26] The evidence is complex, but a few examples will be enough to demonstrate the translator's method of working.[27] Compare, for instance, *Elckerlijc* 648–9:

> U love ic, dat ic dus heb gebracht
> Vroescap, scoonheyt, viif sinnen ende cracht . . .
> ('I praise thee, because I thus have brought
> Wisdom, Beauty, Five Senses, and Strength . . .')

and the corresponding lines, in *Everyman* 679–80:

[21] On the Morality Play in general see R. A. Potter, *The English Morality Play* (London, 1975).

[22] A. Brandl, *Quellen des weltlichen Dramas in England vor Shakespeare* (Strassburg, 1898), p. xxx; M. M. Keiller, 'The Influence of *Piers Plowman* on the Macro Play of *Mankind*', *PMLA* 26 (1911), 339–55; W. R. Mackenzie, 'A New Source for *Mankind*', *PMLA* 27 (1912), 98–105; M. P. Coogan, *An Interpretation of the Moral Play, Mankind* (Washington, 1947), pp. 38–45.

[23] F. A. Wood, '*Elckerlijc–Everyman*: The Question of Priority', *MP* 8 (1910), 293, writes: 'the author of *Everyman* had too little knowledge of the Bible even to translate a play that was based upon it'.

[24] R. W. Zandvoort, *Collected Papers* (Groningen, 1954), pp. 46–7.

[25] Hence his failure to spot wrong line-division in *Elckerlijc*; see J. M. Manly, '*Elckerlijc–Everyman*: The Question of Priority', *MP* 8 (1910), 269–70.

[26] *goodly vision* (*Everyman* 582) is from the Dutch *godlic wesen*, 'divine being'. See J. Conley, 'Aural Error in *Everyman*?' *N&Q* N.S. 22 (1975), 244–5.

[27] The examples are from E. R. Tigg, 'Is *Elckerlijc* Prior to *Everyman*?', *JEGP* 38 (1939), 568–96.

I give thee laud that I have hither brought
Strength, Discretion, Beauty, and Five Wits—lack I nought . . .

Lacking the rhyme *gebracht/cracht*, the English translator has been obliged to use the rhyme-tag 'lack I nought', with the result that the new line is exceptionally long. And compare again *Elckerlijc* 690–1:

Hier in desen aertschen leven
Die heylighe sacramenten seven . . .
('Here in this earthly life
The holy sacraments seven . . .')

and lines 721–2 in *Everyman:*

Here in this transitory life, for thee and me,
The blessed sacraments seven there be . . .

It is impossible to believe that the Dutchman could have found his rhymes simply by removing the tags 'for thee and me' and 'there be . . .' in *Everyman*, so bringing to the end of the line the words 'life' and 'seven', which happen to rhyme in Dutch. Obviously, it is the Englishman who has made the alteration, and the result is the same as before—greater line length. Likewise *god* in *Elckerlijc* becomes *God's magnificence* (line 159), *god almachtich* becomes *the chief Lord of paradise* (line 110), and *den oversten heere* becomes *the highest Jupiter of all* (line 407). The resultant style, surprisingly, is not one which seems heavily padded or over-ornate, but one which is closer to natural speech rhythms and is less strictly confined to a regular verse-form than the Dutch. It is a style well suited to expressing strong emotion, and has been justly admired.

The narrative framework of both *Elckerlijc* and *Everyman* can be traced to the oriental folktale of the Faithful Friend, the earliest version of which is in *Barlaam and Josaphat*, a collection of stories for medieval preachers to use as illustrative material in their sermons.[28] Adaptations of the tale crop up in a variety of places. Typically, it tells of a man who is in dire trouble and is summoned to appear before the king; having approached his friends, he finds that those he has loved best soon desert him, whereas the one he has loved least, agrees to go with him, plead for him, and support him to the end. The *Elckerlijc* dramatist, or someone before him, adapted this basic story in such a way as to reflect the widespread preoccupation with death in the later middle ages. The fascinated revulsion which people felt, and the moral purpose to which the fear of death was put, are reflected in the many tombs and memori-

---

[28] See the appendix. Another version, printed by Caxton, is in Cawley, pp. xviii–xix.

als of the time which feature a horribly realistic skeleton or cadaver and an inscription reminding that all men must eventually follow the same course. The adaptor utilized certain specific conventions connected with death, such as: the idea that human life is a pilgrimage to the next world;[29] the Dance of Death, a macabre procession in which gleeful skeletons dance along to the grave with men of all ranks (but usually high temporal and spiritual lords) as their unwilling partners;[30] and the church's teaching about the art of dying, which was that 'holy dying' can only be achieved with proper preparation and through the institutions of the catholic church.[31] Add to these the other, more general, influences to which all the Morality Plays were subject, and it is easy to appreciate that the apparent simplicity of *Everyman* is only achieved by a skilful distillation of a highly complex theological, philosophical, and ethical background.

Mundus et Infans also has a direct source, in the late fourteenth- or early fifteenth-century poem *The Mirror of the Periods of Man's Life*.[32] In eighty-two eight-line stanzas it presents the one-hundred-year life of a Mankind figure in the form of an overheard dialogue between Man himself and a whole array of characters, including the World, the seven deadly sins, the seven virtues, Conscience, Wanhope, and Man's Good and Bad Angels. Eleven ages are mentioned, despite the fact that at least one version is called in the manuscript 'The Seven Ages', and seven is the number in Jaques's speech in *As You Like It;* in the *Mirror* the ages are from birth to seven, fourteen, twenty, and then at ten-year intervals to one hundred. Conscience is the chief virtue, but his advice is rejected by Man until the last age, when Good Hope and Good Faith (equivalent to Perseverance in the play) drive out Wanhope (Despair). There can be little doubt that the poem is the direct source of the play, for apart from the general similarities there are numerous verbal parallels and wholesale borrowings.[33] The first stanza, equivalent to *Mundus et Infans* 28–35, will demonstrate this sufficiently:

How mankind doth begin
Is wonder for to scrive [describe] so.

[29] See *Everyman* 68n.
[30] See J. M. Clark, *The Dance of Death in the Middle Ages and the Renaissance* (Glasgow, 1950); P. Tristram, *Figures of Life and Death in Medieval English Literature* (London, 1976).
[31] See N. L. Beaty, *The Craft of Dying* (New Haven and London, 1970); Cawley, pp. xvi–xvii.
[32] ed. F. J. Furnivall, *Hymns to the Virgin and Christ* (London, EETS O.S. 24, 1867), pp. 58–78.
[33] MacCracken, op. cit., 486–96.

In game he is begotten in sin.
The child is the mother's deadly foe;
Ere they be fully parted on twain
In peril of death ben both two.
Poor he come the world within,
With sorrow and poverty out shall he go.[34]

The words are those of the narrator, which in the play are adapted
for the child; but since most of the poem is dialogue already,
adaptation was not difficult. The dramatist has drastically reduced
the number of characters, seventeen of which appear in a single
stanza of the poem (lines 33–40); reduced the debate element
between the vices and virtues, focusing attention on Man himself;
and has compressed the seven deadly sins and other vices into
the single character Folly, who does not appear in person in the
poem but whose name may have been suggested by a number
of references in the dialogue. In addition he has expanded
the didactic roles of Conscience and Perseverance, especially in
expounding the doctrines which lead to salvation, which are merely
brief references in the poem. Poem and play rely on the traditional
concept of the ages of man, which can be traced to Aristotle;[35] in
time, the number of ages expanded from three usually to seven,
and the scheme was put to increasingly didactic use, culminating in
the Moralities, after which, as Jaques's speech illustrates, the
moralizing element diminished.

MANKIND

The play begins with a sermon, in which Mercy preaches that the
only means of salvation lies in him. All Mercy's speeches are a
valuable key to the play's meaning, and this opening address estab-
lishes several themes which are to unfold—the foundation of
mercy in Christ's sacrifice on the cross; the importance of good
works as an antidote to temptation; and the nearness of the Last
Judgment, at which every man shall render account of himself. But
Mercy's sermonizing is not allowed to run over-long, for he is
mockingly interrupted by the chief vice, Mischief. At this point, a
leaf is tantalizingly missing from the manuscript, but probably in
the lost portion a challenge was thrown down, Mischief boasting of
his power to win man to sin, and Mercy asserting his trust in the
strength of good. When the text resumes, the three worldly vices,
Newguise, Nowadays, and Nought, who burst upon the scene,

---

[34] My modernization of Furnivall's text.
[35] See B. S. Lee, 'A Poem "Clepid the Sevene Ages"' in *An English Miscellany
Presented to W. S. Mackie*, ed B. S. Lee (Cape Town, 1977), pp. 72–92.

extend the mockery of Mercy to physical abuse, and by the time they swagger off, singing, they have provided Mercy with a vivid *exemplum* and the audience with a taste of the struggle which is about to be enacted.

Enter Mankind, a plain, honest, English farming man. Unlike Everyman, he knows from the start the difference between right and wrong, and laments the fact that his carnal desires often get the better of his spiritual aspirations. Mercy acts as his confessor and warns him that life is a perpetual struggle against wickedness. As if to demonstrate the fact, the vices once again interrupt, and Mercy, his catechizing complete, must leave Mankind to face the test.

Mankind's answer to the vices, who try to distract him by singing a scatological 'Christmas song' (with the help of the audience) and by mocking his meagre plot of arable land, is to beat them off with his spade. With the worldly vices thus repulsed by the instrument of honest labour, Mischief is obliged to call up the devil Titivillus, who succeeds with guile where the less subtle distractions of the others have failed. Stealthily he puts difficulties in Mankind's way, stealing his grain, placing a board in the ground to make digging difficult, diverting him from his prayers, and finally convincing him that Mercy has been hanged. Forgetful of the constant availability of Mercy, Mankind turns to a life of wickedness, leaving Mercy distraught but, like the good shepherd, assiduously seeking the lost one of the flock. The full extent of the evil plan is laid bare when the vices induce in Mankind *wanhope,* the belief that he can never be saved. He is about to hang himself, when Mercy enters with a whip, like Christ in the temple, and the wrongdoers flee. By now Mankind has been tested enough, and the play ends with his return to the fold, and with a fuller explanation of the Three Enemies—the World, the Flesh, and the Devil—against which every man must constantly be on his guard.

Mankind has been dismissed as 'ignorant, corrupt [and] probably degenerate', 'the least learned of the moralities', and a 'sham morality'; and the comic scenes have been described as 'vulgar but not funny' and 'irrelevant and unrelated to the dramatic needs of the play'.[36] But recent studies have shown that, on the contrary, the play is theologically and philosophically subtle, while actual performances have proved that, of all the Moralities, *Mankind* relies most heavily upon bawdy humour and violent action to make its moral point. The audience, for instance, is unwittingly drawn into singing the Christmas song (lines 332–43), little realizing

---

[36] The changing opinions about *Mankind* are usefully summarized by L. K. Stock, 'The Thematic and Structural Unity of *Mankind*', *SP* 72 (1975), 386–7.

the filthy words it will be forced to sing after the first line. And by paying for the privilege of seeing the 'abominable presence' of Titivillus it shares in the devil's own evil. Mercy's chastening words of rebuke to Mankind, therefore, are meant for everyone.

The dramatist probably achieved much of the effect of 'sport', 'game', and misrule by borrowing from Folk Plays current in his day. In the absence of any surviving early Folk Play text (which is hardly surprising, since the script, if any, is one of the least important features of a genuine traditional play), we can only rely on the evidence of the Mummers' Plays of the eighteenth century and later. Features which Mankind shares with them include the taking of a collection; the use of a familiar character (Titivillus) whose arrival is anticipated by the audience and deliberately built up by the actors; the singing and dancing; the fight (with the spade); the proximity of the audience, through whom the vices several times elbow their way; the seasonal, winter-time nature of the play; and the place of performance (perhaps an inn or a private house or any other suitable place where there was an audience willing to pay). Individually these features can be found outside the Mummers' Plays, but their combined presence suggests a substantial folk influence, notwithstanding the fact that Mankind is in other respects a very 'learned' play.[37]

No single character epitomizes the blend of comic and serious so much as Titivillus. Widely popular in European literature and drama, he is first encountered by name in fourteenth-century sources, but can be recognized in unnamed demons of a century earlier.[38] Sermons mention the sack in which he collects the syllables and syncopated words and verses which clerics steal from God by lazily omitting them from their prayers, and also the roll of parchment on which he writes down idle chatter spoken in church. Both these sides of him are present in the Towneley *Last Judgment* play. But in *Mankind* his traditional roles are played down, and his traditional attributes are reduced to a mantle of invisibility and a net (lines 529–31). In *Mankind* he is more a deceitful whisperer, backbiter, and cheat, the agent of Mankind's lapse into sin than merely the recorder of it.

It is easy to see why this figure should have become so popular that the players of *Mankind* were able to take a money collection before allowing the audience to see him. The very sermons from

---

[37] W. K. Smart, '*Mankind* and the Mumming Plays', *MLN* 32 (1917), 21–5; N. Denny, 'Aspects of the Staging of *Mankind*', *Medium Ævum* 43 (1974), 252–63.
[38] M. Jennings, 'Tutivillus: The Literary Career of the Recording Demon', *SP* 74 (1977), *Texts and Studies*, 5.

which he was born continued to remind of his lurking presence, and
a physical image of him was promoted through church carvings,
wall-paintings, and pictures in manuscripts.[39] In *Mankind* he
introduces an element of grotesque comic humour, which was
accentuated no doubt by a suitable costume, a large false head or
mask, probably much roaring and shouting offstage, and by the
performance of some gratuitous sleight of hand (lines 569–72).
Yet, for all this, his role is a deadly serious one, for just as Newguise, Nowadays, and Nought typify the physical sloth to which
Mankind's honest industry is the effective remedy, Titivillus is the
instigator of the spiritual sloth which proves to be the chink in
Mankind's armour. The theme of sloth is kept in mind partly by
Mercy's admonitions (e.g. line 300), partly by example (for the
audience would have been quick to recognize Mankind's industry
as *busyness*, the virtue by which sloth is repelled), and partly by
allusion to the Book of Job.[40] The Old Testament tells that Job was
afflicted by deprivation and disease but refused to curse God; he
was therefore taken as the epitome of patience in adversity. The
book of Job is quoted verbatim in line 228, and the suggestion that
Mankind, like Job, will soon be tested is introduced in line 283.
Shortly afterwards (lines 285–92) comes the open encouragement
to 'see the great patience of Job in tribulation' and 'follow the steps
of him', and Mankind writes down a text adapted from Job (line
321) to help him think of higher things as he sets to work 'to eschew
idleness' (line 329). So when the worldly vices try to lead him
astray, he is well prepared to drive them off. Physical sloth has been
kept at bay, and Mankind wins round one. But by exploiting his
susceptibility to spiritual sloth Titivillus succeeds where the others
have failed. Mankind becomes impatient of his agricultural toil, he
lets his bodily needs interrupt his prayers, and is foolish enough to
believe the rumour that God's mercy is no longer available to him.
The suicide, by which the devil would have won his soul for ever, is
only prevented in the nick of time by the emphatic reassertion that
Mercy is alive and well—both for Mankind and all men.

It is no accident that Titivillus, whose duties included the
recording of whispers, lies, false oaths, and idle talk, is so promi-
nent in a play concerned with language and the issue of verbal
sin.[41] *Mankind* is not alone among the Moralities in making a

---

[39] See M. D. Anderson, *Drama and Imagery in English Medieval Churches* (Cambridge, 1963), pp. 173–7.
[40] The relevance of the Book of Job to *Mankind* is dealt with in Stock, op. cit.,
388–407; Neuss, 'Active and Idle Language', pp. 46–9. See also L. L. Besserman,
The Legend of Job in the Middle Ages (Cambridge, Mass., and London, 1979).
[41] See K. M. Ashley, 'Titivillus and the Battle of Words in *Mankind*', *Annuale
Mediaevale* 16 (1975), 128–50.

character's style of speech reflect his spiritual condition;[42] but what is an incidental feature in other plays is a major theme in *Mankind*, and the polarity of good and evil is objectified in the contrast between good speech ('talking delectable', 'lovely words', 'doctrine monitory') and bad speech ('idle language', 'language . . . large' [vulgar], 'leasings' [lies], 'derision', and 'japing'). Mercy, who is 'approximate to God, and near of his counsel', understandably provides a model of the elevated style. However pompous and irritating this may seem to a present-day reader, there is little doubt that in the fifteenth century the richly aureate diction exemplified in Mercy's speeches had status. Certainly the lofty sentiments and polysyllabic Latinate words ('obsequious', 'remotion', 'participable', 'premeditation') are a delight to Mankind, who exclaims (line 225):

> Oh, your lovely words to my soul are sweeter than honey!

Mankind's own style of speech reflects his changing inward condition; when he is in a state of grace he speaks in four-line stanzas reminiscent of Mercy's own speech:

> O Mercy, my suavious solace and singular recreatory,
> My predilect special, ye are worthy to have my love!
> For, without desert and means supplicatory,
> Ye be compatient to my inexcusable reprove.   (lines 870-3)

but when he is with the worldlings he adopts their characteristic tail-rhyme stanza and a lower style.

The theme of good and bad language is linked to the recurrent agricultural imagery in the play. This imagery emanates from Mankind himself, who is both an ordinary farmer and a symbol of honest toil. In his simple endeavours to serve God through labour he calls to mind the archetypal 'plain Christian', Piers Plowman, and through the symbolism of his spade and his opening allusions to earth and clay he reminds us of Adam and of man's burden of original sin. The farming context gives point to several references to the corn which will be saved and the chaff which will be burnt (lines 43, 50, 54-63, 180, 185), and it is these which bring us back to the question of language: idle words are the chaff which at the Last Judgment will cause their users to be cast into the fire of hell, for then, as Mercy explains, we must all appear before God and

> for every idle word we must yield a reason.   (line 173)

Mercy is not only eloquent: he is incapable of expressing a base sentiment, and remains adamantly silent when Nowadays chal-

---

[42] e.g. in *Everyman* 581ff the protagonist's eloquent style reflects his improved spiritual state.

lenges him to express a scatological couplet in Latin (lines 129–34).[43] For their part the vices show no such abstemiousness. They mock Mercy's language, calling it 'to-gloried' (line 772) and 'full of English Latin' (line 124), and their own speech is replete with excretory and sexual allusions, which, translated into Latin, they laughingly characterize as 'eloquence' (lines 142, 150). Almost every speech they make proclaims them to be damned. Their jibes, curses, jingles, mockery, invective, and chit-chat are not merely comic diversion, any more than their horseplay is a sop to 'popular' taste, 'unrelated to the dramatic needs of the play'.[44] _Mankind, more than any other Morality, instructs by example._ Mercy preaches, and the wild debauchery of the comic scenes provides the living text.

EVERYMAN

Everyman portrays a man's struggles in the face of death to raise himself to a state of grace so that he may die a holy death, secure in the expectation of everlasting life. In restricting the action so narrowly to the last phase of life it is exceptional among the Moralities, for other plays depict at least a portion of the protagonist's unreformed life, and in many it forms the major part. In _Nature_ and _Mundus et Infans_ the time-span covers almost the whole period of life, while in _The Castle of Perseverance_ we follow the progress of the soul even beyond the grave. The normal pattern gives the dramatist scope to present life as a conflict between virtue and vice, and to show fallen man indulging in all sorts of sinful pursuits, which we have every reason to imagine the public enjoyed seeing. The _Everyman_ dramatist, therefore, has forfeited the element of bawdy humour, but has gained for his play in the process an awe-inspiring seriousness.

Everyman's dissolute life is reflected in the people and possessions he has held dear and to whom he first turns in his necessity. In a sense, these embody the seven deadly sins which he has

---

[43] cf. also lines 183–4, 736; also Man's question in _Nature_, p. 94: '_Quid est Latinum propter le stewys?_' and Youth's taunt to Charity (_Youth_ 113–22):

What! methink ye be clerkish,
For ye speak good gibb'rish . . .

followed by the question:

Why do men eat mustard with salt fish?

[44] See Stock, op. cit., 387.

allowed to master him.[45] God has prepared for this in his opening speech by referring to mankind's use of 'the seven deadly sins damnable', but even without this hint a medieval audience would have been quick to perceive the signs of their influence. Everyman's fine clothes would have instantly introduced implications of pride, and his trust in worldly riches, even to the extent that he offers Death a thousand pounds to 'defer this matter till another day', suggests the sin of covetousness. Fellowship offers to cheer Everyman by feasting and drinking and enjoying the company of women (gluttony and lechery), and speaks of murder as if it has been a regular means of entertainment for Everyman (wrath). All his 'friends' by their unwillingness to go on the journey could be said to exemplify sloth, and Goods, in taking such a delight in Everyman's misfortunes (line 456), exemplifies a recognized form of envy. However, we need not pursue these plausible implications too far, for it would be a mistake to try to reconstruct Everyman's previous conduct from these brief suggestions of his former life. The dramatist is careful to present Everyman as a representative, not as an individually well-realized character, so Everyman does not really *have* a specific past. The references to killing as a means out of the situation are less indicative of a former life than of the facile remedies that first come to mind; they are, on account of their ridiculousness, perhaps the nearest thing in the play to comic relief. Likewise, the bribe Everyman offers Death shows rather his ignorance of the situation than his great wealth, for even the poor are capable, like Everyman, of putting their trust in worldly things.

The plot of *Everyman* is unusual for a Morality Play, but what it teaches is completely in keeping with the others: that because of mankind's fallen state and Adam's original sin, a man is not capable of saving himself through his own efforts; that through the graces earned by Christ's victory on the cross the free gift of salvation is available; that the benefits of the redemption are passed to men through the ministration of the church; and that salvation is possible even for the sinner faced with death so long as he is truly repentant.[46] *Everyman* is again different, though, in laying down an exceptionally detailed course of contrition, confession, absolution, and satisfaction, and in being particularly careful to explain the function of priests in administering the sacraments. But apart from the one 'sermon' on priesthood (lines 732–68), the dramatist conveys his teaching not so much through direct address as

[45] T. F. Van Laan, '*Everyman*: a Structural Analysis', *PMLA* 78 (1963), 468–70.
[46] L. V. Ryan, 'Doctrine and Dramatic Structure in *Everyman*', *Speculum* 32 (1957), 723–4.

through 'simultaneously occurring emotional and doctrinal climaxes', and through an action which 'brings into harmony the natural, dramatic, and theological elements of Everyman's experience'.[47] The first step in Everyman's spiritual regeneration necessitates his learning a few painful lessons. When approached by Death he is in a state of total ignorance, and seems astonished to learn even the truths which are embodied in such proverbial commonplaces as 'Death giveth no warning' (line 132) and 'Tide abideth no man' (line 143). Death is no mere messenger: his more important function is to teach Everyman the facts of life and death, and at one point (line 168) he is so undeathlike as to show signs of emotional involvement. As Everyman learns, so do we, but not so much from Death's words as from our emotional association with Everyman in his plight, and the knowledge that we will all some day be in the same predicament ourselves.

Everyman's first recourse is to the people and things he has loved best, and in the beginning these promise fair. Fellowship is approached first because he and Everyman have been good friends 'in the world' (line 200). Fellowship's reply is predetermined by his very nature; though he will not forsake his friend 'in the way of good company' (line 214), or 'while the day is clear' (line 274), or 'and [if] thou go to hell' (line 232), his bluff heartiness fails to cover the shallowness of his promises, and what Everyman learns is once again encapsulated in a proverb—'In prosperity men friends may find,/Which in adversity be full unkind' (lines 309–10). A proverb also leads Everyman's thoughts to his next hope, his kinsmen, for 'Kind will creep where it may not go' (line 316). The irony is that the proverb has a double-edge: Everyman clearly understands the proverb to mean that 'kind', i.e. 'kin', will help him out; however, the true meaning is that 'kind', i.e. 'human nature', will assert itself in every situation, that is, that Kindred and Cousin will behave in a way which Everyman should have foreseen—by letting him down.[48] Once again, the lesson learned is enshrined in a proverb: 'Fair words maketh fools fain' (line 379), and Everyman now turns to Goods, which proves to be the most damning of all his hoped-for worldly remedies. Everyman has great expectations of his Goods, for he has heard it said that 'Money maketh all right that is wrong' (line 413). Like Fellowship, Goods offers help 'in the world' (line 401), but the lesson Everyman has to learn is expressed in an aphorism which also has a traditional ring about it: 'To thy soul Good [Goods] is a thief' (line 447). An excessive love of possessions not only lets a man down: since it

[47] Ibid., 723.
[48] See *Everyman* 316n.

represents the deadly sin of covetousness, it must also lead to the damnation of the soul.

Everyman, near despair, now seems to reach his lowest point, but, unknown to him, his regeneration has already begun. We notice that from this point onwards he is less inclined to be guided by proverbial lore, the ambivalence of which has hitherto led him astray. The first glimmer of hope comes when, turning to his Good Deeds, he finds her weak and 'sore bound' by his neglect, but willing to help, and with a positive course of action to suggest. Good Deeds has already been anticipated by references in the speeches of God (line 78) and Goods (line 432). Her other names were Alms or Charity, and it was the church's teaching that without charitable works a man could not expect to enter the kingdom of heaven. Charity is the presiding virtue in the play *Youth*, and makes this very point in his opening address:

> There may no man saved be
> Without the help of me . . .
> I am the gate, I tell thee,
> Of heaven, that joyful city.
> There may no man thither come
> But of charity he must have some . . .   (lines 8–19)

But the church also teaches that Good Deeds are of no use to a man in a state of sin, so Everyman has to cleanse himself by penance. To help him in this, Good Deeds introduces her sister, Knowledge, who from this point becomes the principal guide. Knowledge appears to mean 'acknowledgement of one's own sin', though other meanings may be present as well, such as 'understanding'.[49] Everyman's 'understanding' is certainly growing all the time, and it is fitting that he should now be joined by a second set of friends—Discretion, Strength, Beauty, and Five Wits—who this time are aspects of himself, not external things like those to which he turned at first. This second group of characters is an addition to the traditional Faithful Friend narrative. The author of *Elckerlijc*, or someone before him, introduced them only to have them enact a second desertion, so as to make the point that man cannot depend on his own powers any more than he can depend on friends and family in his hour of need. Only Good Deeds goes into the grave with him, and Everyman, now as firm in understanding as he was formerly in ignorance, preaches the final moral:

> Take example, all ye that this do hear or see,
> How they that I loved best do forsake me,
> Except my Good Deeds that bideth truly.   (lines 867–9)

---

[49] See *Everyman* 520n; also Ryan, op. cit., 728–9.

Analysis of the structure of *Everyman*[50] shows that the play is divided into two balanced and complementary parts, almost equal in length. There is a certain inevitable symmetry between the first set of 'friends' and the second, and there are signs that the *Everyman* dramatist recognized this and made changes in his source in order to develop it. From a visual point of view, Goods and Good Deeds are the most clearly related pair, and may both have been present on different sides of the acting area at the start of the performance. Good Deeds lies weakly on the ground, fettered by Everyman's sins, while Goods is equally immobilized by Everyman's excessive love:

> I lie here in corners, trussed and piled so high,
> And in chests I am locked so fast,
> Also sacked in bags—thou mayst see with thine eye
> I cannot stir—in packs low I lie. (lines 394–7)

The translator has made changes in *Elckerlijc* here, for in the Dutch play Elckerlijc's possessions are described as lying discarded and filthy in a heap, the emphasis being not so much on the quantity of riches as on the misuse of them. One of the reasons for the change was probably to differentiate, not without irony, the two 'bound' characters: Goods, the greatest enemy, whom Everyman has loved most, and Good Deeds, the greatest friend, whom he has loved least. Everyman's soliloquy between his encounters with Goods and Good Deeds is the focus of the whole play. Exactly in the middle, it is both the low point for Everyman and the turning point. This is the last of a series of soliloquies which usefully enable Everyman to summarize the action and describe his changing feelings, and which verbally and visually emphasize his increasingly desperate loneliness. Recurrent motifs in these speeches are his short and abortive prayers (lines 192, 304, 378); his constant preoccupation with time (lines 192, 194, 383, 386); and the heavy emphasis on sorrow, pain, sickness, and distress (lines 191, 308, 310). We find the counterparts to these same regularly recurring motifs in the second part of the play in contexts which show that the crisis is gradually being resolved.[51] The desperate, ejaculatory prayers are replaced now by a single, fully-developed plea to God, resting upon sound theological principles, and expressed in elevated language (lines 581–604); the motif of time is also resolved, and as his salvation becomes more certain Everyman becomes more eager to proceed 'without tarrying' (line 651); and pain also changes its meaning, as Everyman rejoices in the self-

---

[50] On this see Van Laan, op. cit.
[51] ibid., 467, 471.

imposed suffering which he now knows is the means by which he will eventually pass beyond the reach of all pain (lines 528, 612, 628).

MUNDUS ET INFANS

Mundus et Infans is more typical of the Morality genre than either *Mankind* or *Everyman*. It has particular affinities with *Hick Scorner* and *Youth*, all three showing an arrogant, bullying protagonist led astray by a single evildoer (Folly, Hick Scorner, Riot) into a life of debauchery, before the inevitable conversion to virtue. The sins of fallen mankind are conventional enough—robbery, drinking, wenching—but they are placed in a specific London context, and one wonders whether these three roughly contemporary plays reflect a real alarm at the spread of hooliganism and a real concern for the lack of respect shown to the clergy.[52] The focusing of evil predominantly upon the one figure is clearly a stage in the development of the character who after the middle of the sixteenth century became known as 'the Vice'. The beginnings can be seen in Mischief in *Mankind*, the leader of the wordly vices Newguise, Nowadays, and Nought (though he is strangely ill-characterized and is quite overshadowed by Titivillus). In *Mundus et Infans* there are two centres of evil—the World and Folly. The World cannot be called a vice, for evil resides in what he represents, not what he does: but Folly is an engaging villain, who mocks virtue and plots Manhood's downfall, and is firmly in the Vice tradition, even though the verbal skill, cunning ingenuity, and overriding centrality of the true Vice to the plot are not yet apparent in him.[53]

In presenting almost the whole of man's life, *Mundus et Infans* resembles the early Moralities *Nature* and *The Castle of Perseverance*, and is the complete antithesis of *Everyman*, the action of which seems to take place within a single day. The author, in adapting his source for perhaps as few as two actors, has drastically simplified the time reference, reducing the eleven ages of the source poem to effectively no more than three—youth, manhood, and age. Within the period of youth he has more skilfully presented references to the passage of time; for example, he has made Wanton refer retrospectively to his seventh year (in contrast to the mechanical 'When the child was seven years old . . .' of the poem); he has boldly made Lust and Liking refer to the passing of two years within twelve lines of a single speech (lines 144–55); and he has

---

[52] See D. M. Bevington, *Tudor Drama and Politics* (Cambridge, Mass., 1968), pp. 40–1. Also Lancashire, *Two Tudor Interludes*, pp. 17–95.

[53] See P. Happé, *Tudor Interludes*, pp. 14–15.

logically extended the seven-year stages of youth to twenty-one years (as opposed to the poem's twenty). After this he abandons the mechanical ten-yearly summary of the poem in favour of a more striking presentation of prime-of-life and decrepitude. In addition, he has underlined the progressive stages by adapting the Morality convention of costume change; in entering the 'service' of the World, the Child receives a livery, first as the World's page, then as his squire, then as his knight; grown to Manhood, he remains in this costume for most of the play, though his conduct ironically falls far short of the ideals his knightly status should entail; succumbing to Folly, he puts on the garment of Shame; and when realization dawns and he is given the new name Repentance, his new condition is probably symbolized by yet another new garment, similar to Everyman's 'garment of sorrow'.

One of the main concerns of the dramatist in adapting the *Mirror* was to present the moral teaching more emphatically and to specify a more definite course of repentance and reform. In the poem, man reaches the age of sixty, when he begins to lament his evil ways, at about the half-way point; but he has to drag his way through another forty years of increasing decrepitude before the various stages of despair are overcome and salvation is won. In the play, a better balance is achieved by concentrating on two conversions (the same pattern as in *Nature* and *The Castle of Perseverance*)—an imperfect conversion in middle life and a more complete one in old age. The first provides opportunity for a sermon by Conscience on the Ten Commandments, and the second for a longer exposition by Perseverance of the five inner and outer senses and the Twelve Articles of the Faith. All of these subjects seem to have been suggested by a mere four lines of the *Mirror*:

> The Commandments that God bade,
> That is the lock of heaven gate;
> Seven Works of Mercy, and the Creed,
> These keys shall let me in thereat.[54]

The necessary time and space is gained by sweeping away the clutter of characters who gather round man; to replace them the dramatist has expanded Conscience and the World, and created the new characters Perseverance and Folly from a combination of those suppressed. The course of salvation and damnation is also related more to contemporary conditions in the play—Folly is no abstract vice, but a representative of all that is evil in city

---

[54] Lines 629–32. My modernization.

lowlife, and Conscience is no mere abstraction but an actual preaching friar.[55]

The play also makes its point, less explicitly but every bit as emphatically, by utilizing conventions which for a medieval audience would carry strong moral implications. For example, when Age laments the loss of physical health with the words

Where is my body so proud and prest? (line 795)

this would call to mind the moralizing poetic catalogues of transitory things which begin with the words '*Ubi sunt* . . . ?' (in English 'Where are . . . ?') Even in speeches where there is no apparent reference to time and decay, the images are sometimes so typical as to carry an implicit suggestion of it; so, when the World boasts of the palaces, steeds, and riches which are within his gift, an audience trained to associate these things with impermanence and temporality would be quick to see through the vaunting words. Again, the images of an extensive medieval love literature lie behind Lust and Liking's speech in lines 131–9; but the terms of praise which are normally addressed to the loved one are there arrogantly applied by the speaker to himself

I am as fresh as flowers in May... (line 132)

and the boast that he would be prepared to 'lie in hell till doomsday' for the sake of love is, in the context of a moral play, surely meant to be damning. So too are the proud speeches of the World and Manhood, which, with their calls for silence, demands for respect, threats, curses, and extravagant imbecility, would remind the audience of tyrants such as Herod and Pharaoh in the Mystery Plays. In adapting such conventions the author shows some sensitivity; for instance, the World threatens poverty where the tyrants threaten physical abuse, and offers his followers riches where the others offer peace;[56] and Manhood, through the World-like boasting of his own speech, shows that he has fully become the World's man, even to the extent that he has assumed the manners and mannerisms of his master.

The stanza-patterns of *Mundus et Infans* are difficult to make sense of. The four-line pattern of the first 51[57] lines suddenly gives way to the eight-line tail-rhyme stanza, which thereafter predomi-

---

[55] Only the triple recapitulation of the plot (lines 767–85, 829–45, 961–70) seems overlaboured; contrast this with the stage-by-stage summary in the first half of *Everyman*, which is integral and emphatic.

[56] See G. C. Britton, 'Language and Character in some Late Medieval Plays', *Essays and Studies* N.S. 33 (1980), 2–4.

[57] A line is missing in stanza 7.

nates, with occasional lapses into the four-line and other forms. Departure from the norm is used at times to round off a speech (lines 518–20) or for other special effect (lines 699–701). In contrast to the lack of concern apparent in all this, the speeches are internally well organized, and the playwright appears to have deliberately tried to differentiate his characters as fully as possible by using different syles. The two enemies of man are emphatically distinguished, the World's ornate and alliterative extravagance contrasting with Folly's colloquial informality, ingratiating terms of address, and heavy use of initial asseveration. The two friends of man are also distinguished, the flowery, rather Latinate diction of Perseverance contrasting with the extreme simplicity of what is spoken by Conscience. But it is in connection with the Mankind figure that changes of style are put to best effect. The speech of the Child upon entry has all the grace of innocence; it is plain, ordered, and dignified, and the combined use of both past and present tense emphasizes the poise of the Child as he stands at the threshold of the world. When he assumes the name Wanton, the change in his speech is characterized by 'I can' and 'I will'; most of his speech is a catalogue of new-found talents, in which the expletives ('Aha!' 'Yea!') and the demands for attention ('See!', 'Here!', 'Lo!') show a childish excitement. Lust and Liking's speech is full of 'I am'; alliteration (moderately used by the Child and only very little by Wanton) becomes emphatic. In Manhood's speech in lines 237–87 (his longest in the play), 'I have' becomes important, as Manhood, at the peak of his worldly powers, recounts his achievements; hyperbole and heavy alliteration are everywhere apparent. Under instruction by Conscience, Manhood's curses and interjections are gradually replaced by increasingly earnest questions; so, when he promises to reform, his conversion does not come as a complete surprise. Yet despite his firm promise to Conscience, his counter-conversion to Folly does not seem strange, for a *crise de conscience* is evident in another lengthy speech (lines 490–520); the lack of alliteration marks this soliloquy as reflective, rather than passionate, but the fluctuations of style (quite apart from the contradictory points of view expressed) show that Manhood does not have the settled resolution of a firm convert. Genuine reform comes, however, when Age brings man to his second childhood; Age's speeches are a long list of past errors and present indignities, and only through Perseverance's timely intervention is the language of despair modified to the language of resignation.

In adapting the *Mirror*, the dramatist may not have had an entirely free hand, for he has reduced it to a play which, bearing in mind the contemporary practice of doubling, demands no more than two players; this is exceptionally few, and there may have been special reasons for casting it in this way.[58] If we accept that the play was written with only two actors in mind then certain implications need to be borne in mind. One is that, since the protagonist is on stage for most of the time, one player would have to play all the other parts himself, vices and virtues alike. As Bevington has pointed out,

> The unavoidable effect upon structure created by such an arrangement is clear: the opposite members in the struggle cannot be brought face to face with one another. Man must be exposed first to good and then to evil.[59].

The need to make one character disappear in order that another may appear probably explains the total suppression of the World after line 236 and the fact that Conscience passes the care of Age's soul to his 'brother' Perseverance, instead of sharing it with him. But the author has made a virtue of necessity, for it is theologically and psychologically apt that perseverance in the expectation of mercy should follow the stirrings of conscience, and quite appropriate that the World should disappear when Manhood has become so like him as to have no further need of him. Folly, too, may be a happy product of necessity, for he represents vice much more emphatically than the troupe of evil figures in the *Mirror*. Furthermore, the playwright shows some ingenuity in offsetting the restrictions of a small cast by making constant reference to characters like Covetise 'mine own fellow' and 'my brother, Lechery' who never actually appear, and by creating an illusion of expansiveness by giving one character several names.

STAGING

Morality Plays are remarkable for their mobility, so it is not surprising that the three plays have few special staging needs, even to the extent that they require no actual 'stage' other than a space amongst the spectators (the 'place') which it was the established practice of medieval and Tudor plays to utilize.[60] Specific locations were either represented by structures set about the 'place' (like *Everyman*'s House of Salvation, perhaps),[61] or were left to the imagination (aided by the judicious use of a few symbolic props, such as Mankind's spade).[62] The lack of a special set means, for instance,

[58] See Bevington, *From 'Mankind' to Marlowe*, pp. 116–24.
[59] ibid., pp. 117–18.
[60] See R. Southern, *The Medieval Theatre in the Round* (London, 1957), pp. 17–88.
[61] See *Everyman* 540 and note.
[62] See *Mankind* 352–60n.

that Everyman can be shown entertaining his kinsmen at one moment, and approaching his grave at another; and that Mankind can be indoors when he talks to Mercy (line 209), and digging in his field shortly afterwards (line 328), without ever having left the acting area. The absence of a raised stage also encourages a *rapport* between players and spectators which is one of the most attractive features of the Moralities.

In addition to the House of Salvation, *Everyman* requires a grave, and a high place for God and the angel;[63] all other action is unlocalized. Properties mentioned are Death's dart, Everyman's account books, the boxes and bags of Goods, the scourge, and the crucifix. The only costumes mentioned are Everyman's fine clothes and his 'garment of sorrow'; the woodcut illustrations in A and B are probably not reliable evidence of actual staging. Allowing for the practice of doubling, the seventeen speaking parts could be taken by ten players, or perhaps less.[64]

The title-page of *Mundus et Infans* shows the World enthroned under a canopy,[65] and this is probably how we are to envisage him as the play begins. The throne recalls the seat of the World in *The Castle of Perseverance*, which, according to the contemporary staging diagram of that play, is erected on a 'scaffold', which acts as a home base for the World and his followers. In *Mundus et Infans*, the World probably retires to his seat during the soliloquies of the Child, Wanton, and Lust and Liking, and only withdraws completely when Manhood has attained sufficient worldliness to take over from him. Other than the throne, there is no particular set requirement. Without taking references to halls and other buildings too literally (lines 12, 121, etc), we should probably think in terms of indoor performance and an evening or night-time setting (line 525). A number of internal allusions with Christmas associations (such as that to Stephen, line 260) may indicate that *Mundus et Infans* was first written as a Christmas play.[66] The few properties mentioned are Wanton's playthings, gold, silver, and a sword (given to Manhood), the weapons with which Manhood and Folly fight, and Folly's drink and staff. The various costumes by which the ages of man are distinguished are mentioned in lines 30, 45, 67, 268–70, but changes were probably also made with every alteration of the protagonist's name.[67] Conscience is referred to several times

---

[63] The use of a high place to represent heaven was normal in medieval drama, and is most clearly seen in the Mystery Plays.

[64] J. M. Wasson, 'Interpolation in the Text of *Everyman*', *Theatre Notebook* 27 (1972–73), 14–20, argues for as few as seven.

[65] See fig. 3.

[66] Lancashire, p. 97.

[67] See *Mundus et Infans* 641–2n.

as a friar, and Folly seems to be dressed in the rags and tatters of a tinker.[68] The play can be acted by as few as two players, but Southern suggests more, arguing that a child actor would have taken the part of man as far as the beginning of Manhood (line 215), and would then have left the acting area to hand over his part, and perhaps his costume, to an adult;[69] certainly, the Child's remark

I am a child, as you may see (line 30)

suggests either a child actor or that a great deal was left to the imagination.

Mankind is more problematic, not because its staging is more complicated, but because opinion is divided as to the time, place, acting company, and audience for which the play was intended.[70] All the evidence is internal. The time-setting is winter (lines 54, 323), but it is not clear whether it is Christmas, as implied by the 'Christmas song' (line 332), or Shrovetide, the pre-Lenten period of merrymaking, when the playing of football (cf. line 732 and note) was one of the ways of enjoying a final fling before the austerities to come. Certain Lenten themes, such as the Ash Wednesday text of line 321, seem to imply Shrovetide, for Lent itself would not have been a time for plays. Various places of performance have been suggested—notably inns, innyards, and the halls of private houses. On balance, an interior setting seems a little more likely, but the allusions to place need not be taken literally, and out-of-doors performance also seems possible.[71] The 'passing round of the hat' has often been taken to imply that the actors were an itinerant professional troupe, but this in itself does not exclude the possibility of the players being a group of local amateurs. As the subtleties of the play have been increasingly realized, the old view that it was intended for 'rural or village audiences'[72] has given way, and it is now recognized that the many Latin citations, puns, and witty mistranslations would be lost on the uneducated.[73] In all, *Mankind* has something for everyone, for the 'sovereigns that sit' and the 'brothern that stand right up' (line 29), for the workman, the yeoman (line 333), the gentleman—even the cleric. Its very

---

[68] See *Mundus et Infans* 537–8n.

[69] R. Southern, *The Staging of Plays before Shakespeare* (London, 1973), pp. 130–5.

[70] For a variety of views see Smart, pp. 306–8; Eccles, pp. xlii–xliii, 217; Denny, op. cit., 252–63; Southern, *The Staging of plays before Shakespeare*, pp. 21–45, 143–5. L. M. Clopper, '*Mankind* and its Audience', *Comparative Drama* 8 (1974), 347–55..

[71] Southern, loc. cit., is excessively literal in arguing that *Mankind* was written to be staged in the great hall of a private house.

[72] Bevington, *From 'Mankind' to Marlowe*, p. 16.

[73] See especially Clopper, op. cit., 349–50.

ambiguity of time and place suggests a play which could be adapted to suit a variety of occasions, and this, together with its generally high quality, seems to support the idea of a professional touring group.

The properties mentioned are a spade, bag of grain, paper, writing instrument, and rosary (for Mankind); a net, board, and weeds (for Titivillus); a scourge (for Mercy); a weapon, fetters, dish, plate, rope, and gallows (for Mischief); and a flute, purses, noose, stolen goods, pen, and paper (for the other vices). As for costumes, Titivillus has a large head, Mankind wears a 'side-gown', which is cut down to make a jacket, and Mercy is a 'seemly father', the term probably implying clerical dress. The seven parts can be played by six actors, if one takes the parts of both Mercy and Titivillus.

A NOTE ON THE TEXT

THIS IS A modern-spelling edition, the preparation of which has involved many difficult decisions as to how 'modern' the editor can be without losing too much of the sense and 'feeling' of the original. While not wishing to overload the glosses and explanatory notes, I have tried to be fairly conservative, and have been guided in the case of obsolete words by the preferred form in the *OED*. Older forms are generally kept in rhymes, but in a few instances where this might have seemed obtrusive (e.g. *iournaye*, 'journey' and *than*, 'then') I have used the modern form and recorded the rhyme in a note. Words for which the proposed modernization is only tentative have also been noted. Where a defective rhyme is involved, I have not resorted to conjectural emendation, except in cases in which the regular pattern can be restored by a simple expedient such as the transposition of two words, or, at most, two whole lines. Otherwise lines and stanzas which are deficient in rhyme are left to speak for themselves. Mere literals (minor compositorial errors) are corrected without notice. Glosses are given only for the first occurrence of a word within each play, except that I have occasionally repeated a gloss in cases of possible ambiguity. Latin quotations, numerous in *Mankind* but found also in *Everyman*, have been left in Latin (with regularized spelling where necessary) and translated in the notes. Word-division has been altered to conform with present-day practice (e.g. *a geyn* is printed *again*). Roman numerals are replaced by words, and common abbreviations in the *Mankind* manuscript are silently expanded. Capitalization and punctuation are modern. Capitalization presents a particular problem in the Morality Plays, for a concept such as 'pride' may be personified at one occurrence and not at the next. The ambiguity is deliberately exploited in *Mundus et Infans* 341–489. In cases like this I have reserved initial capitals for clear cases of personification only. Square brackets signify editorial stage directions. There are no original stage directions in *Mundus et Infans*, and only two in *Everyman*. The few and rather random directions in *Mankind* are in either Latin or English; in the case of those in Latin the original is given in the text and a translation of it in a footnote.

Mankind is found in a single manuscript, Washington D.C., Folger Library MS V.a.354 (formerly 5031), ff.122–34r. The same manuscript also contains *The Castle of Perseverance* and *Wisdom*, but the three plays did not originally belong in the same volume. It was from a former owner, the Revd. Cox Macro

(1683–1767), that the plays acquired their common name 'The Macro Plays'. The manuscript of *Mankind* presents greater editorial difficulties than the printed editions in which *Everyman* and *Mundus et Infans* are found, and I have been helped by the availability of a good facsimile by David Bevington, *The Macro Plays* (New York, 1972), which supersedes an earlier one by J. S. Farmer (London and Edinburgh, 1907) for the Tudor Facsimile Texts. The main editions are in: Manly, Vol I; A. Brandl, *Quellen des weltlichen Dramas in England vor Shakespeare* (Strassburg, 1898); F. J. Furnivall and A. W. Pollard, *The Macro Plays* (London, EETS E.S.91, 1904); J. S. Farmer, *'Lost' Tudor Plays* (London, 1907); Eccles; Bevington; J. A. B. Somerset, *Four Tudor Interludes* (London, 1976); Glynne Wickham, *English Moral Interludes* (London, 1976). The standard unmodernized edition is that of Eccles. The manuscript comprises a single first leaf followed by a gathering of twelve. The original second leaf has been lost, for those remaining are numbered i, iii–x in the hand of the original first scribe, with the last four unfoliated. One scribe wrote the first twenty-one pages, a second the last four. There are also several contemporary alterations in a different ink, evidence of supervision or revision; these are too complicated to enumerate in the present edition and can be studied in Bevington's facsimile. Neither scribe observed the common convention of linking rhymed words with brackets, nor is the text set out in stanzas, although the rhyme-scheme itself is stanzaic. I have adopted the same stanza divisions as in the edition of Eccles, except that, in common with most other editors, I have taken 'Nowadays mak proclamacyon', which is written in the margin after line 665, as a stage direction; so my line numeration differs from that of Eccles by one from this point. Mercy speaks mainly in stanzas of four or eight lines *abab, ababbcbc*; Mankind mainly in the same four-line stanza; the vices in tail-rhyme stanzas of eight lines, mostly *aaabcccb*; and Titivillus in a variety of stanzas up to twelve lines long. Irregular stanzas occur beginning at lines 53, 122, 305, 331, 333, 335, 392, 445, 749, and lines are missing in those beginning 147, 202, 631, 686, 771.

Everyman survives in two complete early printed editions and two early fragments: A. San Marino, California, Huntington Library (*STC* 10606), printed by John Skot *c*.1528–29, the complete text in sixteen leaves; the title-page has woodcuts of Everyman and Death, the colophon Skot's device. B. London, British Library (*STC* 10605), the complete text in sixteen leaves printed by Skot *c*.1530–35; the title-page has woodcuts similar to A, and on the verso there are additional woodcuts of six of the characters from the play (see figs 1 and 2); this edition lacks the colophon. C. Oxford, Bodleian Library, Douce fragment (*STC* 10604), the earliest of the four, printed by Richard Pynson *c*.1510–25; it comprises four damaged leaves containing the text from line 683 to the end, plus colophon. D. British Library (*STC* 10603), a fragment of ten leaves of another edition by Pynson, *c*.1525–30, containing lines 305 to the end, plus colophon. A, which is used in the present edition, is considered the best text, for reasons which are set out in detail by W. W. Greg in *Materialien* 28. The same volume of *Materialien* contains transcripts of C and D, while transcripts of A and B respectively are in volumes 4 and 24 (Louvain, 1904, 1909). In the footnotes of the present edition variant readings are given only in the few instances in which A is emended or in which BCD have readings of special interest. After the four early sixteenth-century editions the next to appear, so far as we know, was in T. Hawkins, *The Origin of the English Drama* (Oxford, 1773), Vol I; subsequent editions are very numerous, and a full list may be consulted in C. J. Stratman's *Bibliography of Medieval Drama*. Cawley's is the standard unmodernized edition. In line with all other editions, the present one does not attempt to print the text in stanzas because of the extreme irregularity of the verse-length, verse-forms, and rhymes. This is summarized by Cawley, p. xxvii:

> The number of syllables in a line ranges from four to fourteen. The verse-forms are a welter of couplets and quatrains, together with occasional tail-rhymes, five-, six-, and seven-line stanzas, rhyme-royal stanzas, and octaves. There are more than a hundred imperfect rhymes: some are examples of assonance and some are due to corruption of the original text, but this still leaves several pairs of words which fail to rhyme, as well as end-words without companion rhyme-words.

The unique surviving edition of *Mundus et Infans* (*STC* 25982) is now in the library of Trinity College, Dublin, and was printed (i.e. published), according to the colophon (see fig. 4) by Wynkyn de Worde on 17 July 1522. For the present edition I have used the facsimile by J. S. Farmer (London and Edinburgh, 1909), for the Tudor Facsimile Texts. The other main editions are in: Manly, Vol I, the best unmodernized edition; J. S. Farmer, *Six Anonymous Plays* (London, 1905); E. T. Schell and J. D. Shuchter, *English Morality Plays and Moral Interludes* (New York, 1969). The lines of *Mundus et Infans* vary greatly in length, and there is variety also in the rhyme schemes. I have followed the lead of Manly in printing the text in stanzas, though my own arrangement sometimes differs from his, as does the line-division in a few cases (with the result that this edition has 974 lines to Manly's 979). The most common stanzas are of four lines *abab*, eight lines with tail-rhyme *aaabcccb*, and a nine-line mixture of the two *ababcdddc*. Other stanza types of from three to six lines are found, sometimes for emphasis (e.g. the stanzas beginning at lines 283, 518, 553, 699, 802, 845, 969). Stanzas which are corrupt or not easily explicable occur at 160, 300, 622, 753, 823. Rhymes are frequently defective, and for this reason the stanza patterns cannot be regarded as totally established. There appears to be a line missing from each of the stanzas beginning 25, 100, 668, 702, 787.

FURTHER READING

Ashley, K. M., 'Titivillus and the Battle of Words in *Mankind*', *Annuale Mediaevale* 16 (1975), 128–50.

Bevington, D. M., *From 'Mankind' to Marlowe* (Cambridge, Mass., 1962).

Britton, G. C., 'Language and Character in some Late Medieval Plays', *Essays and Studies* N.S. 33 (1980), 1–15.

Coogan, M. P., *An Interpretation of the Moral Play, Mankind* (Washington, 1947).

Craik, T. W., *The Tudor Interlude* (Leicester, 1958).

Houle, P. J., *The English Morality and Related Drama: a Bibliographical Survey* (Hamden, Conn., 1972).

Kolve, V. A., *'Everyman* and the Parable of the Talents' in *Medieval English Drama*, ed J. Taylor and A. H. Nelson (Chicago and London, 1972), pp. 316–40.

Lancashire, I., 'The Auspices of *The World and the Child*', *Renaissance and Reformation* 12 (1976), 96–105.

Lee, B. S., 'A Poem "Clepid the Sevene Ages"' in *An English Miscellany Presented to W. S. Mackie*, ed B. S. Lee (Cape Town, 1977), pp. 72–92.

MacCracken, H. N., 'A Source of *Mundus et Infans*', *PMLA* 23 (1908), 486–96.

Mackenzie, W. R., *The English Moralities from the Point of View of Allegory* (Boston and London, 1914).

Neuss, P., 'Active and Idle Language: Dramatic Images in *Mankind*' in *Medieval Drama*, ed N. Denny (London, 1973), pp. 40–67.

Potter, R. A., *The English Morality Play* (London, 1975).

Ryan, L. V., 'Doctrine and Dramatic Structure in *Everyman*', *Speculum* 32 (1957), 722–35.

Southern, R., *The Staging of Plays before Shakespeare* (London, 1973).

Spivack, B., *Shakespeare and the Allegory of Evil* (New York and London, 1958).

Stock, L. K., 'The Thematic and Structural Unity of *Mankind*', *SP* 72 (1975), 386–407.

Van Laan, T. F., *'Everyman*: a Structural Analysis', *PMLA* 78 (1963), 465–75.

MANKIND

DRAMATIS PERSONAE

MERCY
MISCHIEF
NEWGUISE
NOWADAYS
NOUGHT
MANKIND
TITIVILLUS

In Orig. ∿

MANKIND

No S.D.'s — No scene divisions
No titles

[*Enter* MERCY]

MERCY

The very Founder and Beginner of our first creation, → *one of us.*
Among us sinful wretches he oweth to be magnified,
That for our disobedience he had none indignation
To send his own son to be torn and crucified;
Our obsequious service to him should be applied,   5
Where he was Lord of all and made all thing of nought,
For the sinful sinner, to had him revived
And for his redemption, set his own son at nought.

It may be said and verified: Mankind was dear bought;
By the piteous death of Jesu he had his remedy.   10
He was purged of his default, that wretchedly had
    wrought,
By his glorious passion, that blessed lavatory.
O sovereigns, I beseech you your conditions to rectify, → *as attention*
And with humility and reverence to have a remotion   *is wandering?!*
To this blessed prince that our nature doth glorify,   15
That ye may be participable of his retribution.

I have be the very mean of your restitution;
Mercy is my name, that mourneth for your offence.
Divert not yourself in time of temptation,

→ *bold announcement of char.*

2 *oweth to be magnified* ought to be praised
5 *obsequious* obedient
6 *Where* Inasmuch as
9 *dear bought* redeemed at a high price
11 *He ... wrought* He (mankind) who had behaved despicably was cleansed of his
    sins
12 *lavatory* purifier (i.e. Christ)
13 *sovereigns* gentlefolk (the audience)
13 *conditions* habits
14 *remotion* recourse
15 *that our nature doth glorify* who glorifies our nature (by having become man)
16 *participable of his retribution* entitled to share in his reward
17 *be the very mean* been the true means
19 *Divert not yourself* Do not go astray

7–8 *For ... nought* And, in order that the sinner (mankind) might be redeemed and
    born again, he gave up his own son.

That ye may be acceptable to God at your going hence.   20
The great mercy of God, that is of most preeminence,
By mediation of our Lady—that is ever abundant
To the sinful creature that will repent his negligence.
I pray God, at your most need that Mercy be your defend-
     ant.

In good works I advise you, sovereigns, to be perseverant,   25
To purify your souls that they be not corrupt,
For your ghostly enemy will make his avaunt,
Your good conditions if he may interrupt.

O ye sovereigns that sit and ye brothern that stand right
     up,
Prick not your felicities in things transitory!   30
Behold not the earth, but lift your eye up!
See how the head the members daily do magnify.
Who is the head? Forsooth, I shall you certify:
I mean our Saviour, that was likened to a lamb;
And his saints be the members that daily he doth satisfy   35
With the precious river that runneth from his womb.

There is none such food, by water nor by land,
So precious, so glorious, so needful to our intent;
For it hath dissolved mankind from the bitter bond

---

22 *mediation* ed (medytacyon MS)
22 *that* i.e. the great mercy of God, etc.
27 *avaunt* boast
29 *brothern* fellows (i.e. the common people)
30 *Prick not your felicities in* Do not fasten your hopes on
36 *womb* side
37 *by water nor by land* i.e. anywhere
37 *land* ed (londe r.w. bonde MS)
38 *needful to our intent* necessary for our purpose

---

27 *your ghostly enemy* the enemy of your soul, the devil (cf. *Everyman* 334, *Mundus et Infans* 751).
29 *sovereigns ... brothern* There seems to be a distinction here between the different classes comprising the audience. These are perhaps analogous to the seated spectators and the 'groundlings' of the Shakespearian theatre (cf. *Hamlet* III.ii.12).
32–8 The image of Christ as the head and the church as the body can be traced back to Colossians 1:18. I Corinthians 12:12–31 elaborates the idea of individual Christians as members (parts of the body). Lines 36–8 refer to the blood of Christ as the sacrament. See Smart, p. 56.

Of the mortal enemy, that venomous serpent, 40
From the which God preserve you all at the Last Judg-
    ment!
For, sickerly, there shall be a strait examination.
'The corn shall be saved, the chaff shall be brent'—
I beseech you heartily, have this premeditation,

[*Enter* MISCHIEF] → relieve from Latinate sermon
↳ shows that we are just

MISCHIEF

I beseech you heartily, leave your calcation,   as evil 45 as them.
Leave your chaff, leave your corn, leave your dalliation;   Mischief
Your wit is little, your head is mickle; ye are full of predica-
    tion.   legitimises our
But, sir, I pray you this question to clarify: boredom.
Mish-mash, driff-draff,
Some was corn and some was chaff.   Tension. 50
My dame said my name was Raff.
Unshut your lock and take an ha'penny!

42 *sickerly* certainly
42 *there* ed (the MS)
42 *strait* strict
46 *dalliation* chatter
47 *predication* preaching
48 *you* ed (om MS)
49 *Mish ... draff* ed (Dryff draff mysse masche MS)

---

40 *the mortal enemy, that venomous serpent* The devil, who assumed the form of a
   serpent to tempt Adam and Eve, is the 'mortal' enemy who brings about spiritual
   death.
43 *The corn ... brent* The first reference to an important theme in the play, deriving
   from Matthew 3:12 and Luke 3.17. Cf. lines 50, 54–63, 180, 185.
45 *calcation* trampling (?). Eccles suggests 'threshing' (cf. line 43), but this sense is
   not attested in *MED* or *OED*. A possible emendation is *calculation*.
47 *Your wit is little, your head is mickle* This is reminiscent of the Fool or Beelzebub
   in present-day Mummers' Plays, who sometimes begins: 'Here come I; ain't
   been yit,/Big head and little wit'. See W. K. Smart, *MLN* 32 (1917); also cf.
   Tilley, H 245; Whiting, H 226.
49–52 Mischief seems to have seized upon line 43 (cf. line 50) as the basis for an
   echoic nonsense-rhyme which mocks and interrupts Mercy's preaching. For
   situational and verbal parallels compare the interruption of Felicity by Fancy in
   Magnificence 248–55, and for similar rhymes see Iona and Peter Opie, *Children's
   Games in Street and Playground* (Oxford, 1969).

MERCY

Why come ye hither, brother? Ye were not desired.

MISCHIEF

For a winter-corn thresher, sir, I have hired.

And ye said the corn should be saved and the chaff should
be fired.   55

And he proveth nay, as it sheweth by this verse:

'Corn *servit bredibus*, chaff *horsibus*, straw *firibusque*'.

This is as much to say, to your lewd understanding,

As: the corn shall serve to bread at the next baking;

—'Chaff *horsibus, et reliqua*'—   60

The chaff to horse shall be good provent;

When a man is forcold the straw may be brent;

And so forth, *et cetera*.

MERCY

Avoid, good brother; ye ben culpable

To interrupt thus my talking delectable.   65

MISCHIEF

Sir, I have neither horse nor saddle;

Therefore I may not ride.

MERCY

Hie you forth on foot, brother, in God's name!

MISCHIEF

I say, sir, I am come hither to make you game.

---

54 *winter-corn* grain sown in autumn or winter
55 *fired* burnt
56 *he* i.e. the author of the verse
58 *lewd* ignorant
60 *et reliqua* and the rest
61 *provent* fodder
62 *forcold* very cold
64 *Avoid* Go away
69 *make you game* have fun with you

---

57 *Corn ... firibusque* doggerel Latin meaning 'Corn serves for breads, chaff for
horses, and straw for fires'. Mischief parodies Mercy's exegesis by explaining
this 'text' to the people (line 58 presumably refers to the audience).

Yet, bade ye me not to go out in the devil's name,   70
And I will abide.

MERCY

[*Here a leaf is missing from the manuscript. Enter* NEWGUISE *and* NOWADAYS *with* NOUGHT, *whipping him to make him dance*]

[NEWGUISE]

And ho, minstrels! Play the common trace!
[*To* NOWADAYS] Lay on with thy baleys till his belly brest!

NOUGHT

I put case I break my neck—how then?

NEWGUISE

I give no force, by Saint Anne!   75

NOWADAYS

Leap about lively! Thou art a wight man!
Let us be merry while we be here.

NOUGHT

Shall I break my neck to show you sport?

NOWADAYS

Therefore ever beware of thy report.

72 *the common trace* a simple, basic dance tune
73 *baleys* whip
73 *brest* bursts
74 *I put case* Suppose
74 *then* ed (than r.w. anne, man MS)
75 *I give no force,* I care not
76 *wight* nimble

70–1 *Yet ... abide* i.e. since you did not invoke the devil (Mischief's master) in bidding me go out, I will remain. In medieval legends of *Noah* the devil is able to enter the Ark when Noah invokes his name in swearing at his wife. See Rosemary Woolf, *The English Mystery Plays* (London, 1972), pp. 136–7.
71 s.d. The contemporary folio numbers show that a single leaf has been lost, and with it about 70 lines of text. Lines 98, 111, and 417–8 imply that in the missing portion Mercy spoke of Newguise, Nowadays, and Nought, and argued with Mischief. Wickham, *English Moral Interludes*, p. 5 speculates that Nought enters dressed in a pantomime bearskin with a detachable head, and adds: 'This image suffices to equate the Vices at the outset with loutish thugs whose spiritual kinship lies with the lower animals rather than civilized men'.
72 *minstrels* Music was a feature of all periods of medieval drama, both secular and religious.
75 *Saint Anne* mother of the Virgin Mary.
79 An uncharacteristically weak line if it means only 'Watch what you say'. Perhaps there is play on *report*, which can mean 'talk' or 'musical sound', referring to the music for the dance.

NOUGHT
> I beshrew ye all! Here is a shrewd sort!   80
> Have thereat, then, with a merry cheer!

Here they dance. MERCY *saith:*

MERCY
> Do way! Do way this revel, sirs, do way!
NOWADAYS
> Do way, good Adam, do way?
> This is no part of thy play.
NOUGHT
> Yes, marry, I pray you, for I love not this revelling!   85
> Come forth, good father, I you pray;
> By a little ye may assay!
> Anon, off with your clothes, if ye will, pray!
> Go to, for I have had a pretty scuttling!

MERCY
> Nay, brother, I will not dance.   90
NEWGUISE
> If ye will, sir, my brother will make you to prance.
NOWADAYS
> With all my heart, sir, if I may you advance!
> Ye may assay by a little trace.
NOUGHT
> Yea, sir, will ye do well,
> Trace not with them, by my counsel;   95
> For I have traced somewhat too fell!
> I tell, it is a narrow space!

> But sir, I trow of us three I heard you speak.

---

80 *beshrew* curse
80 *Here is a shrewd sort* Here is a bad lot (i.e. What villains you are)
83 *good Adam* old man
87 *By . . . assay* You may have a little try yourself
89 *a pretty scuttling* a great deal of prancing about
92 *if I may you advance* if you allow me to help you (with my whip)
94 *will ye do well* if you wish to do well
95 *Trace* Dance
96 *fell* ferociously
97 *I tell . . space* I declare, they allow a small area (for dancing)

NEWGUISE
Christ's curse have therefore, for I was in sleep.
NOWADAYS
And I had the cup ready in my hand ready to go to meat;   100
Therefore, sir, curtly, greet you well.
MERCY
Few words, few and well set!
NEWGUISE
Sir, it is the new guise and the new jet:
Many words, and shortly set—
This is the new guise, every deal.   105

MERCY
Lady help! How wretches delight in their sinful ways!
NOWADAYS
Say nought again the new guise nowadays;
Thou shall find us shrews at all assays!
Beware! Ye may soon lick a buffet!
MERCY
He was well occupied that brought you, brether!   110
NOUGHT
I heard you call 'Newguise, Nowadays, Nought'—all these
three together;

---

99 *have* ed (hade MS)
100 *And* ed (A MS)
100 *meat* dine
101 *curtly* in short
103 *jet* fashion
104 *shortly set* rudely, curtly put
106 *sinful* ed (sympull MS)
107 *again* against
108 *shrews* ed (schewys MS)
109 *lick a buffet* feel a blow
110 *brether* ed (brethern MS) brothers

99–100 The sleeping and eating may be meant to suggest the sins of sloth and
gluttony. See M. D. Anderson, *Drama and Imagery in English Medieval
Churches*, pp. 66–70.
102 *Few ... set* said ironically, as line 110.
108 *shrews at all assays* difficult people to deal with in every encounter (with the
additional meaning of 'rogues').

Physically + verbally abuse Mercy — but he is not angry

MANKIND

If ye say that I lie, I shall make you to slither.
Lo, take you here a trippet!   *[Trips him]*

MERCY

Say me your names. I know you not. *good device for announcing*
NEWGUISE   *names — but they've been on*
Newguise I.   *stage for ages by now!*
NOWADAYS

                I Nowadays.
NOUGHT

                        I Nought.   115
MERCY

By Jesu Christ, that me dear bought,
Ye betray many men!
NEWGUISE

Betray? Nay, nay, sir, nay, nay!
We make them both fresh and gay.
But, of your name, sir, I you pray,   120
That we may you ken.

MERCY

Mercy is my name and my denomination—
I conceive ye have but a little favour in my communication.
NEWGUISE

Ey, ey, your body is full of English Latin!
I am afeard it will brest.   125
'*Pravo te*', quod the butcher unto me
When I stole a leg o' mutton.
Ye are a strong cunning clerk.
NOWADAYS

I pray you heartily, worshipful clerk,
To have this English made in Latin: 130

'I have eaten a dishful of curds,
And I have shitten your mouth full of turds'.

113 *trippet* trip
119 *fresh and gay* fashionable and colourful
121 *ken* know
125 *afeard it will brest* afraid it will burst
128 *strong cunning clerk* very knowledgeable cleric, scholar

---

124 *English Latin* Latinate diction, on which see above, pp. xxiii–xxv.
126 *Pravo te* I curse you. Eccles quotes *Ortus Vocabulorum* (1500), which glosses
  the verb 'to shrewe'.

Now, open your satchel with Latin words,
And say me this in clerical manner!
Also, I have a wife (her name is Rachel);   135
Betwix her and me was a great battle;
And fain of you I would hear tell
Who was the most master.

NOUGHT
Thy wife Rachel, I dare lay twenty lice!
NOWADAYS
Who spake to thee, fool? Thou art not wise!   140
Go and do that longeth to thine office:
Osculare fundamentum! _so rude to Mercy, would a mod. audience accept this?_
NOUGHT
Lo, master, lo, here is a pardon belly-met;
It is granted of Pope Pocket: _mind you — would they understand it?_
If ye will put your nose in his wife's socket
Ye shall have forty days of pardon.   145

MERCY
This idle language ye shall repent!
Out of this place I would ye went.
NEWGUISE
Go we hence all three, with one assent.
My father is irk of our eloquence! _— hardly surprising note!_ 150

---

134 *clerical manner* scholarly style, Latinate diction
137 *fain* gladly
141 *that longeth to thine office* what you should be doing, what is natural to you
142 *Osculare fundamentum* Kiss my (or his) backside
145 *socket* i.e. vagina
150 *irk* tired

---

133 *open your satchel with Latin words* an anti-scholastic joke, cf. *Hick Scorner*
789–90: 'Nay, I have done, and you lade out Latin with scoops!/But therewith
can you clout me a pair of boots?' Likewise, the Miller in Chaucer's *Reeve's Tale*
challenges the two Cambridge students to make his sleeping accommodation
larger by their 'argumentes' (*Canterbury Tales*, A 4123–4).
143–6 The selling of pardons, or indulgences, was practised by the medieval
papacy for the considerable income it brought. On the activities of pardoners,
whose job it was to purvey them, see Chaucer's *Canterbury Tales* A 669–714, C
329–968. The significance of the imaginary Pope Pocket is discussed above, p.
xiv. *belly-met* (MS bely mett) has not been convincingly explained; the most
likely meaning is 'to the measure of the belly, full and satisfying' (Eccles).

[handwritten margin note: Do we still feel with N/N/N now — ought to do so — but they i.e.e so awful to Mercy — wd. have to be carefully organised + staged in order to retain our sympathies. for plot reasons?]

Therefore, I will no longer tarry.
God bring you, master, and blessed Mary,
To the number of the demonical friary!

NOWADAYS

Come wind, come rain,
Though I come never again,   155
The devil put out both your een!
Fellows, go we hence tight.

NOUGHT

Go we hence, a devil way!
Here is the door, here is the way.
Farewell, gentle Geoffrey,   160
I pray God give you good night!   *Exiant simul. Cantent*

MERCY

Thanked be God we have a fair deliverance
Of these three unthrifty guests!
They know full little what is their ordinance:
I prove by reason they be worse than beasts: 165

A beast doth after his natural institution:
Ye may conceive, by their disport and behaviour,
Their joy and delight is in derision
Of their own Christ, to his dishonour.

This condition of living, it is prejudicial;   170
Beware thereof! It is worse than any felony or treason.

156 *een* ed (eyn r.w. reyn, ageyn MS) eyes
157 *tight* quickly
158 *a devil way* in the devil's name
161 s.d. *Exiant simul. Cantent* Let them go out together. Let them sing
163 *unthrifty guests* worthless visitors
164 *what is their ordinance* what is their ordained place (in God's creation)
166 *doth ... institution* behaves as his ordained nature requires
170 *prejudicial* harmful

152–3 *God ... friary* May God and the Blessed Virgin Mary hand you over to the
    brotherhood of the devil. Cf. lines 325–6 and note.
159–60 *Here ... Geoffrey* A similar saying is in John Heywood, *Proverbs* (1546):
    'Nowe here is the doore, and there is the wey. And so (quoth he) farewell,
    gentill Geffrey'. This, and other instances of 'gentle Geoffrey', are cited in
    Tilley, G 81; see also D 556; Whiting, G 47. Smart, p. 293, suggests the name
    implies 'a slow, listless man, a procrastinator', and compares *Do-Little* in line
    262.

How may it be excused before the Justice of all,
When for every idle word we must yield a reason?

They have great ease; therefore, they will take no thought.
But how then, when the angel of heaven shall blow the
    trump,   175
And say to the transgressors that wickedly hath wrought,
'Come forth unto your judge, and yield your account'?

Then shall I, Mercy, begin sore to weep.
Neither comfort nor counsel there shall none be had;
But such as they have sown, such shall they reap.   180
They be wanton now, but then shall they be sad.

The good new guise nowadays I will not disallow;
I discommend the vicious guise—I pray have me excused;
I need not to speak of it; your reason will tell it you.
Take that is to be taken, and leave that is to be refused. 185

[*Enter* MANKIND]

MANKIND
Of the earth and of the clay we have our propagation;
By the providence of God thus be we derivate—
To whose mercy I recommend this whole congregation;
I hope unto his bliss ye be all predestinate.

Every man, for his degree, I trust shall be participate,   190
If we will mortify our carnal condition
And our voluntary desires, that ever be perversionate,
To renounce them and yield us under God's provision.

172 *Justice* Judge
183 *discommend* condemn
186 *we have our propagation* we are born
187 *be we derivate* we are derived
190 *for his degree* according to his qualities
190 *be participate* share in it
192 *perversionate* tending to pervert
193 *yield us under* submit ourselves to

173 *for ... reason* Cf. Matthew 12:36–7: 'But I say unto you that every idle word
    that men shall speak, they shall render an account for it in the day of judgment.
    For by thy words thou shalt be justified; and by thy words thou shalt be
    condemned'.
177 *yield your account* present an account of your life. For an elaboration of this
    theme see *Everyman*.
180 *such ... reap* Galatians 6:8.

My name is Mankind. I have my composition
Of a body and of a soul, of condition contrary.   195
Betwix them twain is a great division;
He that should be subject, now he hath the victory.

This is to me a lamentable story,
To see my flesh of my soul to have governance.
Where the good-wife is master the good-man may be sorry.   200
I may both sigh and sob; this is a piteous remembrance.

O thou my soul, so subtle in thy substance,
Alas! What was thy fortune and thy chance
To be associate with my flesh, that stinking dunghill?

Lady, help! Sovereigns, it doth my soul much ill   205
To see the flesh prosperous and the soul trodden under
   foot.
I shall go to yonder man, and assay him I will;
I trust of ghostly solace he will be my boot.

[*Approaches* MERCY]

All hail, seemly father! Ye be welcome to this house.
Of the very wisdom ye have participation.   210

197 *He* The one, i.e. the body
199 *of . . . governance* to have control over my soul
201 *a piteous remembrance* a lamentable thought
202 *subtle* delicate
204 *associate with* joined to
205 *Lady* Our Lady
208 *of . . . boot* he will help me with his spiritual comfort
210 *Of . . . participation* You have access to true wisdom

---

195 *Of a body and of a soul* The dispute between the soul and the body was a
   ubiquitous motif of medieval sermons, and took the form of a war of words in a
   spirited Middle English debate poem. The theme appears in *Pride of Life*
   93–100 and *Perseverance* 3012–20. For discussion of the background see A. C.
   Baugh, *A Literary History of England* (London, 1967), pp. 162–4; Spivack,
   Shakespeare and the Allegory of Evil, pp. 67–9.
200 *Where . . . sorry* No exact parallel has been found for this anti-feminist proverb,
   but for the tradition which lies behind it see R. L. Greene (ed), *The Early
   English Carols* (Oxford, 1977), pp. 241–2, 457–8.
209 *seemly father* Mankind's terms suggest that Mercy is in modest clerical dress.

My body with my soul is ever querelous;
I pray you, for saint charity, of your supportation.

                                          [*Kneels*]

I beseech you heartily of your ghostly comfort.
I am unsteadfast in living; my name is Mankind.
My ghostly enemy, the devil, will have a great disport,   215
In sinful guiding if he may see me end.

MERCY

Christ send you good comfort! Ye be welcome, my friend.
Stand up on your feet, I pray you, arise.
My name is Mercy. Ye be to me full hend.
To eschew vice I will you advise.   220

MANKIND

O Mercy, of all grace and virtue ye are the well—
I have heard tell, of right worshipful clerks,
Ye be approximate to God, and near of his counsel;
He hath institute you above all his works.

Oh, your lovely words to my soul are sweeter than honey!   225

MERCY

The temptation of the flesh ye must resist like a man,
For there is ever a battle betwix the soul and the body.
Vita hominis est militia super terram.

Oppress your ghostly enemy, and be Christ's own knight!
Be never a coward again your adversary.   230
If ye will be crowned, ye must needs fight.
Intend well, and God will be you adjutory.

211 *ever querelous* always at war
212 *saint* holy
212 *supportation* support
216 *sinful* ed (sympull MS)
216 *guiding* conduct
219 *hend* pleasant
222 *of* from
223 *Ye ... counsel* That you are close to God, and privy to his plans
224 *institute* set
230 *again* against
232 *Intend well* Have good intentions
232 *you adjutory* helpful to you

228 *Vita ... terram* The life of man upon earth is a warfare (Job 7:1).

Remember, my friend, the time of continuance; *Life is as short*
So help me God, it is but a cherry-time!   *as the cherry harvest*
Spend it well; serve God with heart's affiance.   235
Distemper not your brain with good ale nor with wine.

be moderate.

'Measure is treasure'. I forbid you not the use.
Measure yourself ever; beware of excess.
The superfluous guise I will that ye refuse,
When nature is sufficed anon that ye cease.   240

If a man have an horse, and keep him not too high,
He may then rule him at his own desire:
If he be fed over-well, he will disobey,
And, in hap, cast his master in the mire.

[*Enter* NEWGUISE, NOWADAYS *and* NOUGHT *at a distance. They mimic* MERCY, *and disturb his counselling*]

NEWGUISE
Ye say true, sir; ye are no faitour.   245
I have fed my wife so well till she is my master!
I have a great wound on my head, lo! and thereon lieth a
    plaster—
And another there I piss, my peson.

---

233 *the time of continuance* the duration of man's life
235 *affiance* trust
237 *I ... use* I do not forbid you to touch them (ale and wine)
237–8 *Measure is ... excess* ed (written as one line in MS)
238 *Measure yourself ever* Always be moderate
239–40 *The ... cease* I wish you to avoid excess, and stop as soon as natural bodily
     requirements are satisfied
244 *in hap* perhaps
245 *faitour* deceiver
248 *there* where

---

234 *cherry-time* The brief time of the cherry harvest. The fair, or festival, which
     was held at this time was a common symbol of worldly transience. Cf. 'This
     world nis but a chirie feire' and other instances cited in *MED*.
237 *Measure is treasure* proverbial (cf. *Oxford Proverbs*, p. 520; Tilley, M 805;
     Whiting, M 461). The character Measure expands on this in *Magnificence*
     121–5, and the most recent editor of that play has called it (p. 22) 'the thesis of
     Magnificence'.
241 *keep him not too high* does not spoil him by over-rich feeding (too many oats and
     not enough grass) which would produce excessive spirit.
248 *peson* a weighing instrument in the form of a staff with balls attached, whence a
     vulgar term for 'penis'.

And my wife were your horse, she would you all to-ban.
Ye feed your horse in measure; ye are a wise man! 250
I trow, and ye were the king's palfreyman,
A good horse should be geason.

MANKIND

Where speaks this fellow? Will he not come near?

MERCY

All too soon, my brother, I fear me, for you!
He was here right now—by him that bought me dear!— 255
With other of his fellows; they can much sorrow.

They will be here right soon, if I out depart.
Think on my doctrine; it shall be your defence.
Learn while I am here; set my words in heart.
Within a short space I must needs hence. 260

NOWADAYS

The sooner the liefer, and it be even anon!
I trow your name is Do-little, ye be so long fro home.
If ye would go hence, we shall come everychone,
Mo than a good sort.
Ye have leave, I dare well say; 265
When ye will, go forth your way.
Men have little dainty of your play,
Because ye make no sport.

NOUGHT

Your pottage shall be for-cold, sir; when will ye go dine?
I have seen a man lost twenty nobles in as little time; 270
Yet it was not I, by Saint Quentin!
For I was never worth a potful of worts sithen I was born.

249 *And* If
249 *you all to-ban* thoroughly curse you
251 *palfreyman* stable attendant
252 *geason* scarce
256 *can* know (how to bring about)
257 *out depart* go away
258 *doctrine* instruction
261 *The ... anon* The sooner the better, if it is straight away
262 *trow* believe
262 *fro* from
263 *everychone* everyone
264 *Mo than a good sort* more than a great company (i.e. in large numbers)
267 *dainty of* liking for
269 *Your pottage shall be for-cold* Your broth will be stone cold
272 *worts* cabbage
272 *sithen* since

My name is Nought; I love well to make merry.
I have be sithen with the common tapster of Bury.
And played so long the fool that I am even very weary;   275
Yet, shall I be there again tomorn.

[*Exeunt* NEWGUISE, NOWADAYS *and* NOUGHT]

MERCY

I have much care for you, my own friend;
Your enemies will be here anon; they make their avaunt.
Think well in your heart, your name is Mankind;
Be not unkind to God, I pray you; be his servant.   280

Be steadfast in condition; see ye be not variant.   *ye/you jumbled.*
Lose not through folly that is bought so dear.
God will prove you soon, and, if that ye be constant,
Of his bliss perpetual ye shall be partner.

Ye may not have your intent at your first desire.   285
See the great patience of Job in tribulation;
Like as the smith trieth iron in the fire,
So was he tried by God's visitation.

He was of your nature and of your fragility.
Follow the steps of him, my own sweet son,   290
And say, as he said, in your trouble and adversity:
'*Dominus dedit, Dominus abstulit; sicut sibi placuit, ita factum
    est. Sit nomen Domini benedictum*'.

---

275 *And* ed (A MS)
276 *tomorn* ed (to morow MS)
280 *unkind* unnatural
282 *that is bought so dear* that which has been purchased, redeemed at so high a price
     (i.e. the soul)
283 *prove* test, make trial of
286 *in* ed (& MS)

---

274 *the common tapster of Bury* has never satisfactorily been explained. The allusion
     may have been topical and specific.
286–92 *See the great patience of Job ... benedictum* This is the most explicit of several
     references to Job (see also lines 228, 321, and above, p. xxiii). Job was smitten
     by a succession of disasters, but refused to curse God, and was regarded,
     therefore, as a model of long-suffering patience. His resignation to divine
     providence is summarized in line 292: 'The Lord gave, and the Lord hath taken
     away. As it hath pleased the Lord so is it done. Blessed be the name of the Lord'
     (Job 1:21).
287 *trieth* refines (a technical term), cf. *OED*: 'To separate (metal) from the ore or
     dross by melting; to refine, purify by fire'. Job 23:10 refers to trying gold in the
     fire. When applied to persons, as in line 288, *try* means 'put to the test'.

Moreover, in special I give you in charge,
Beware of Newguise, Nowadays, and Nought!
Nice in their array, in language they be large;   295
To pervert your conditions all their means shall be sought.

Good son, intromit not yourself in their company.
They heard not a mass this twelvemonth, I dare well say.
Give them none audience; they will tell you many a lie.
Do truly your labour, and keep your holy day.   300

Beware of Titivillus—for he loseth no way—
That goeth invisible and will not be seen.
He will round in your ear, and cast a net before your eye.
He is worst of them all, God let him never theen!

If ye displease God, ask mercy anon, ⟶ *always mercy*   305
Else Mischief will be ready to brace you in his bridle.
Kiss me now, my dear darling. God shield you from your
      fon.
Do truly your labour, and be never idle.
The blessing of God be with you, and with all these
      worshipful men!   [*Exit*]

293 *give you in charge* command you
295 *Nice* Extravagant
295 *large* vulgar
296 *your* ed (ther MS)
297 *intromit* introduce
298 *this* ed (thi MS)
301 *for* ed (fo MS)
301 *loseth no way* wastes no opportunity (to lead people astray)
303 *round* whisper
303 *eye* ed (eyn r.w. wey MS)
304 *theen* thrive, prosper
306 *brace* fasten
307 *shield* ed (schede MS)
307 *fon* enemies
309 *these worshipful men* i.e. the audience

300 *keep your holy day* observe the sabbath (cf. *Mundus et Infans* 427).
301 On Titivillus, the devil who collects idle words and carelessly-spoken prayers,
    see above, pp. xxii–xxiii.

MANKIND
    Amen, for saint charity, amen!   310

Now, blessed be Jesu, my soul is well satiate
With the mellifluous doctrine of this worshipful man.
The rebellion of my flesh, now it is superate.
Thanking be God of the cunning that I can.

Here will I sit, and title in this paper   315
The incomparable estate of my promition. [*Sits and writes*]
Worshipful sovereigns, I have written here
The glorious remembrance of my noble condition,

To have remorse and memory of myself. Thus written it is,
To defend me from all superstitious charms: 320
'*Memento, homo, quod cinis es, et in cinerem reverteris*'.
    [*He makes the sign of the cross, and takes up his spade*]
Lo! I bear on my breast the badge of mine arms.

               [*Enter* NEWGUISE]

---

311 *satiate* satisfied
312 *mellifluous* sweet as honey
313 *superate* under control
314 *of the cunning that I can* ed (of the commynge that I kam MS) for the knowledge
      I have acquired
315 *title* write
316 *The ... promition* The incomparable status which is promised to me (in heaven)

---

321 *Memento ... reverteris* 'Remember, O man, that you are dust, and to dust you
      will return', a text for Ash Wednesday and a common inscription on fifteenth-
      century tombs and memorials, adapted from Job 34:15. Mankind uses it as a
      memento mori, a reminder of the inevitability of death which will help him keep
      his mind on his spiritual welfare.
322 *badge of mine arms* What exactly Mankind means is not clear. It could be a
      crucifix he is wearing, or the note he has just written, marked perhaps with a
      cross (see Smart, p. 295); or perhaps he merely makes the sign with his hand,
      typical at the start of a piece of work. The cross as a badge of arms goes back to
      the Emperor Constantine's vision of it, when he heard the words: 'In this sign
      you shall conquer'.

NEWGUISE

The weather is cold; God send us good fires!
'Cum sancto sanctus eris, et cum perverso perverteris'. ‖
'Ecce quam bonum et quam jocundum', quod the devil to the   325
    friars,
'Habitare fratres in unum'.

MANKIND

I hear a fellow speak; with him I will not mell.
This earth, with my spade, I shall assay to delve.
To eschew idleness, I do it mine own self.   330
I pray God send it his foison!

[*Enter* NOWADAYS *and* NOUGHT *through the audience*]

NOWADAYS

Make room, sirs, for we have to be long!
We will come give you a Christmas song.

NOUGHT

Now, I pray all the yeomanry that is here
To sing with us, with a merry cheer.   335

[*Sings*] It is written with a coal, it is written with a coal ...
[NEWGUISE *and* NOWADAYS *make the audience sing after him*]

NEWGUISE *and* NOWADAYS

It is written with a coal, it is written with a coal ...

---

327 *mell* meddle
328 *assay to delve* try to dig
330 *foison* abundance
331 *be long* been away for a long time
335 *coal* piece of charcoal

---

324 *Cum ... perverteris* 'With the holy thou wilt be holy, and with the perverse thou
     wilt be perverted' (adapted from Psalms 17:26–7, AV 18:26–7).
325–6 *Ecce ... unum* 'Behold, how good and pleasant it is for brethren to dwell
     together in unity' (Psalms 132:1, AV 133:1). Mischief is trying to distract
     Mankind by making a joke at the expense of the friars, whose name means
     'brothers' (Latin *fratres*), by implying they belong to the brotherhood of devils.
     The orders of friars were the butt of many jokes, and came in for much abuse on
     account of their supposed malpractices (see Chaucer's description in *Canter-
     bury Tales* A 208–69).
329 *To eschew idleness* See above, p. xxiii.

NOUGHT

He that shitteth with his hole, he that shitteth with his hole
...

NEWGUISE *and* **NOWADAYS**

He that shitteth with his hole, he that shitteth with his
hole ...

NOUGHT

But he wipe his arse clean, but he wipe his arse clean ...

NEWGUISE *and* **NOWADAYS**

But he wipe his arse clean, but he wipe his arse clean ...   340

NOUGHT

On his breech it shall be seen, on his breech it shall be
seen ...

NEWGUISE *and* **NOWADAYS**

On his breech it shall be seen, on his breech it shall be seen.

        Cantant omnes

Holyke, holyke, holyke, holyke, holyke, holyke!

NEWGUISE

Ey, Mankind, God speed you with your spade!

I shall tell you of a marriage: 345

I would your mouth and his arse, that this made,

Were married junctly together!

MANKIND

Hie you hence, fellows, with braiding!

Leave your derision and your japing!

I must needs labour; it is my living.   350

NOWADAYS

What, sir? We came but late hither.

---

339 *But* Unless
341 *breech* breeches, trousers
343 s.d. *Cantant omnes* All sing
346 *his arse, that this made* the arse of the man who composed this song
347 *married junctly* firmly joined
348 *braiding* reproach
351 *We came but late hither* We have only just come

---

343 *Holyke* is probably a distortion of 'holy', with perhaps also the meaning
'hole-lick', and other vulgar connotations.

mocking small land + crop

Shall all this corn grow here
That ye shall have the next year?
If it be so, corn had need be dear,
Else ye shall have a poor life!   355
NOUGHT

Alas, good father! This labour fretteth you to the bone.
But, for your crop I take great moan.
Ye shall never spend it alone;
I shall assay to get you a wife.

How many acres suppose ye here, by estimation?   360
NEWGUISE

Ey, how ye turn the earth up and down!
I have be, in my days, in many good town,
Yet saw I never such another tilling!
MANKIND

Why stand ye idle? It is pity that ye were born!
NOWADAYS

We shall bargain with you, and neither mock nor scorn: 365
Take a good cart in harvest, and load it with your corn—
And what shall we give you for the leaving?

NOUGHT

He is a good, stark labourer; he would fain do well.
He hath met with the good man Mercy, in a shrewd sell.
For all this, he may have many a hungry meal.   370

356 *fretteth you* wears you down
357 *I take great moan* I am very sad
358 *spend it* use it up
368 *stark* strong
369 *He ... sell* It was a bad moment when he met the good man Mercy

352–60 The mockery of Mankind's small piece of land (and its inevitably small yield) would be all the more pointed if some device such as a small rectangle of cloth were used to symbolize it. Such an expedient would be in the staging tradition of the mystery plays, for which the account books of the Coventry Cappers list among the props 'halfe a yard of rede sea' (Bevington, p. 322), and would establish the location as now out-of-doors, though shortly before (line 209) presumably the same acting area had represented the interior of Mankind's house.

367 *the leaving* what is left when a large cart has carried away the main crop, i.e. nothing. The mockery of Mankind's meagre livelihood continues.

Yet—will ye see?—he is politic!
Here shall be good corn—he may not miss it.
If he will have rain, he may over-piss it!
And, if he will have compass, he may over-bless it
A little with his arse, like ... [*Makes a rude gesture*]   375

MANKIND

Go and do your labour—God let you never thee!—
Or with my spade I shall you ding, by the holy Trinity!
Have ye none other man to mock, but ever me?
Ye would have me of your set.
Hie you forth lively, for hence I will you drive!   380
                    [*Strikes them with his spade*]

NEWGUISE

Alas, my jewels! I shall be shent of my wife!

NOWADAYS

Alas! And I am like never for to thrive,
I have such a buffet!

MANKIND

Hence, I say, Newguise, Nowadays, and Nought!
It was said beforn, all the means should be sought   385
To pervert my conditions, and bring me to nought.
Hence, thieves! Ye have made many a leasing!

NOUGHT

Marred I was for cold, but now am I warm!
Ye are evil-advised, sir, for ye have done harm.
By Cock's body sacred, I have such a pain in my arm   390
I may not change a man a farthing!

                    [MANKIND *kneels*]

---

374 *compass* compost, manure
374 *over-bless it* cover it with dung
377 *ding* strike
379 *set* company
381 *jewels* testicles
381 *I ... wife* I shall be of no use to my wife (sexually)
382 *And ... thrive* I too am likely to be ruined for life
385 *should* ed (xull MS)
387 *leasing* lie

---

390 *Cock's* God's (a common perverted form cf. line 612). The reference is both to
Christ's human form and to the sacrament, which Catholics believe is transformed into the body of Christ in the mass. Swearing by Christ's body was
likened to torturing him anew (cf. Chaucer, *Canterbury Tales*, C 472–5,
629–60).

MANKIND
Now I thank God, kneeling on my knee!
Blessed be his name! He is of high degree.
By the subsidy of his grace that he hath sent me,
Three of mine enemies I have put to flight.   395
                              [*Holds up his spade*]
Yet, this instrument, sovereigns, is not made to defend
David saith: '*Nec in hasta, nec in gladio, salvat Dominus*'.
NOUGHT
No, marry, I beshrew you; it is *in spadibus*!
Therefore, Christ's curse come on your *headibus*,
To send you less might! *Exiant* [*all but* MANKIND]   400

MANKIND
I promit you, these fellows will no more come here,
For some of them, certainly, were somewhat too near!
My father, Mercy, advised me to be of a good cheer,
And again my enemies manly for to fight.

I shall convict them, I hope, everychone—   405
Yet I say amiss! I do it not alone;
With the help of the grace of God I resist my fon
And their malicious heart.
With my spade I will depart, my worshipful sovereigns,
And live ever with labour, to correct my insolence.   410
I shall go fetch corn for my land. I pray you of patience;
Right soon I shall revert. [*Exit*]

              [*Enter* MISCHIEF]

394 *subsidy* help
401 *promit* promise
405 *convict* conquer
410 *insolence* pride
412 *revert* return

397 *Nec ... Dominus* David's words to Goliath: 'The Lord saveth not with sword
     and spear' (I Kings 17:47).
398–9 *in spadibus ... headibus* Nought ruefully answers Mankind's Biblical quota-
     tion in doggerel Latin: 'with the spade' (literally plural). *Headibus*, 'head',
     which merely echoes the Latin inflectional ending, is found also in the inter-
     lude *Thersites* (ed. J. S. Farmer, *Six Anonymous Plays*, p. 200).

MISCHIEF

    Alas, alas, that ever I was wrought!
    Alas the while! I am worse than nought!
    Sithen I was here, by him that me bought,   415
    I am utterly undone!
    I, Mischief, was here at the beginning of the game,
    And argued with Mercy—God give him shame!
    He hath taught Mankind, while I have be wane,
    To fight manly again his fon.   420

    For, with his spade that was his weapon,
    Newguise, Nowadays, Nought he hath all to-beaten.
    I have great pity to see them weepen.
    Will ye list? I hear them cry.
    [*Enter* NEWGUISE, NOWADAYS, *and* NOUGHT, *limping.*]
                      Clamant
    Alas, alas, come hither! I shall be your borrow.   425
    Alack, alack! *Ven, Ven*! Come hither—with sorrow!
    Peace, fair babes! Ye shall have an apple—tomorrow.
    Why greet ye so, why?

NEWGUISE

    Alas, master, alas! My privity!

MISCHIEF

    Ah, where? Alack, fair babe, ba me!   430
                  [NEWGUISE *starts to remove his hose*]
    Abide! Too soon I shall it see.

NOWADAYS

    Here, here, see my head, good master!

---

414 *am* ed (om MS)
419 *be wane* been absent
422 *he* ed (om MS)
424 s.d. *Clamant* They wail
425 *borrow* protector
426 *Ven* come (abbreviated Latin imperative)
428 *greet* weep
429 *privity* private parts
430 *ba* kiss

426ff Despite his motherly manner, Mischief's side-comments show how shallow
    his grief really is, as do his drastic proposals for remedy, which are probably
    designed to frighten the others from their pretended ailments (like the false
    begging cripples of *Piers Plowman* B, Passus VI, who are quickly 'cured' with
    the arrival of Hunger). Mischief's lack of real concern contrasts with Mercy's
    heartful grief, lines 733–70.

MISCHIEF

> Lady, help! Seely darling, *ven, ven!*
> I shall help thee of thy pain—
> I shall smite off thy head and set it on again!   435

NOUGHT

> By our Lady, sir, a fair plaster!
>
> Will ye off with his head? It is a shrewd charm!
> As for me, I have none harm;
> I were loath to forbear mine arm!
> Ye play: *In nomine patris*, chop!   440

NEWGUISE

> Ye shall not chop my jewels, and I may!

NOWADAYS

> Yea, Christ's cross! Will ye smite my head away?
> There! Where? On and on! Out! Ye shall not assay—
> I might well be called a fop.

MISCHIEF

> I can chop it off and make it again.   445

NEWGUISE

> I had a shrewd recumbentibus, but I feel no pain.

NOWADAYS

> And my head is all safe and whole again.
> Now, touching the matter of Mankind,
> Let us have an interlection, sithen ye be come hither.
> It were good to have an end.   450

MISCHIEF

> Ho, ho! A minstrel! Know ye any aught?

433 *Seely* Poor (in a commiserative sense)
436 *a fair plaster* a fine remedy (said ironically)
437 *shrewd charm* severe (magical) cure
439 *forbear* lose
441 *and I may* if I can help it
444 *fop* fool
446 *recumbentibus* knock-down blow
449 *interlection* consultation
450 *It ... end* It would be a good thing to bring the matter to a satisfactory conclusion

---

440 *In nomine patris, chop* 'In the name of the father' (a quick prayer) ... chop (even quicker amputation). This and line 443 were presumably accentuated with appropriate gestures.
451 *A minstrel* Mischief has the sudden idea of calling up Titivillus (presumably after a pause for the consultation mentioned in line 449).

NOUGHT

I can pipe in a Walsingham whistle, I, Nought, Nought.

MISCHIEF

Blow apace! and thou shall bring him in with a flute.

[NOUGHT *plays to attract* TITIVILLUS]

TITIVILLUS [*Offstage*]

I come, with my legs under me!

MISCHIEF

Ho, Newguise, Nowadays! hark, ere I go: 455
When our heads were together, I spake of *si dedero*.

NEWGUISE

Yea, go thy way! We shall gather money unto,
Else there shall no man him see.

[*To the audience*] Now, ghostly to our purpose, worshipful
    sovereigns,
We intend to gather money, if it please your negligence,   460
For a man with a head that is of great omnipotence.

NOWADAYS

Keep your tail in goodness, I pray you, good brother!
He is a worshipful man, sirs, saving your reverence.
He loveth no groats, nor pence of tuppence;
Give us red royals, if ye will see his abominable presence. 465

---

453 *Blow apace* Play forthwith
453 *him* i.e. Titivillus
457 *unto* for the purpose (of inducing Titivillus to appear)
459 *ghostly to our purpose* to effect our supernatural plan (of raising the devil)
461 *is* ed (on MS)
462 *tail* tally, account (of the money collected)
463 *He* i.e. Titivillus

---

452 *Walsingham whistle* probably a cheap whistle of a type sold to the 'tourists' who
    visited the famous shrine of Our Lady of Walsingham.
456 *si dedero* literally 'if I give ...', the implication being that something will be
    expected in return (see Smart, pp. 296–7). The same expression is used in
    Perseverance 879. The collection of money which now takes place is the first
    known instance in an English play.
460 *your negligence* is a comic distortion of 'your reverence'.
461 *a head that is of great omnipotence* Titivillus probably wore a grotesque mask or
    false head. His popularity as a comic figure is shown by the taking of the
    collection at this point.
464–5 *groats ... pence of tuppence ... red royals* 'Groats' and 'coins worth tuppence'
    were of much less value than the newly-introduced gold 'royals'. 'Red' is a
    traditional epithet for gold.

NEWGUISE

Not so! Ye that mow not pay the ton, pay the tother.
> [*They take a collection*]

At the good-man of this house first we will assay.
God bless you, master! Ye say us ill, yet ye will not say nay.
Let us go by and by, and do them pay.
Ye pay all alike; well mote ye fare!   470

NOUGHT

I say, Newguise, Nowadays, *estis vos pecuniatus?*
I have cried a fair while, I beshrew your pates!
> [NOWADAYS *calls* TITIVILLUS]

NOWADAYS

Ita vere, Magister, come forth now your gates.
He is a goodly man, sirs. Make space, and beware!

> [*Enter* TITIVILLUS, *with net*]

TITIVILLUS

Ego sum dominantium dominus, and my name is Titivillus.   475
Ye that have good horse, to you I say *'caveatis!'*
Here is an able fellowship to trice hem out at your gates!

466 *mow ... tother* cannot pay the one, pay the other
468 *us* ed (as MS)
469 *by and by* in and out (of the audience)
469 *do* make
471 *estis vos pecuniatus?* are you well off? (i.e. have you collected enough?)
472 *cried* begged
472 *I beshrew your pates* curse your heads
472 *pates* ed (patus r.w. pecuniatus, gatus MS)
473 *Ita vere, Magister* So indeed, Master
473 *gates* way
476 *caveatis* watch out
477 *Here ... gates* Here is a company of men (Mischief and the others) well able to snatch them from your gates

---

467 *good-man of this house* Either 'the master of this household' or 'the host of this inn', depending on the acting location. They go on to imply that he is cursing them under his breath (for asking for money), but will not refuse (for fear of being shown up in public).
470 *Ye ... fare* all of you are paying up; good luck to you! (words of encouragement said while the collection is in progress).
475 *Ego sum dominantium dominus* I am Lord of Lords (cf. Deuteronomy 10:17 and Apocalypse 19:16), a title also claimed by Pilate in the Towneley play of *The Talents* (ed. M. Rose, *The Wakefield Mystery Plays* (New York, 1969), p. 431).

Ego probo sic: (*Loquitur ad* NEWGUISE) Sir Newguise, lend
   me a penny.

NEWGUISE

I have a great purse, sir, but I have no money.

                          [*Empties his purse*]

By the mass, I fail two farthings of an ha'penny;   480
Yet had I ten pound this night that was.

TITIVILLUS

(*Loquitur ad* NOWADAYS) What is in thy purse? Thou art a
   stout fellow.

NOWADAYS

The devil have the whit! I am a clean gentleman!
I pray God I be never worse stored than I am!
It shall be otherwise, I hope, ere this night pass.   485

TITIVILLUS

(*Loquitur ad* NOUGHT) Hark now! I say thou hast many a
   penny.

NOUGHT

Non nobis, Domine, non nobis, by Saint Denny!
The devil may dance in my purse for any penny;
It is as clean as a bird's arse!

[TITIVILLUS *discovers and confiscates the collected money from
                behind* NOUGHT'*s back*]

TITIVILLUS

[*To the audience*] Now I say yet again, *caveatis*!   490
Here is an able fellowship to trice hem out of your gates!

---

478 *Ego probo sic* I demonstrate it (their dishonesty) thus
478 s.d. *Loquitur ad* NEWGUISE He speaks to NEWGUISE
480 *I ... ha'penny* I'm two farthings short of a ha'penny (i.e. I've nothing)
481 *this night that was* last night
483 *The devil have the whit* May the devil take the little I have (i.e. nothing)
483 *the whit* ed (qwyll MS)
483 *clean* poor, penniless (cf. present-day 'cleaned-out')
484 *stored* provided for
487 *Non* ed (No MS)
490–1 cf. lines 476–7

---

487 *Non ... nobis* Not to us, O Lord, not to us (Psalms 113:1, second set of verses,
     AV 115:1).
488 *The devil ... penny* traditional (cf. *Oxford Proverbs*, p. 180; Tilley D 233;
     Whiting, D 191; Smart, p. 297).
489 *clean as a bird's arse* a traditional simile (cf. Tilley, B 391: 'as bare as a byrdes
     arse'; Whiting, B 317).

Now I say, Newguise, Nowadays, and Nought,
Go and search the country—anon it be sought,
Some here, some there—what if ye may catch aught.

If ye fail of horse, take what ye may else.   495
NEWGUISE

Then speak to Mankind for the recumbentibus of my
jewels!
NOWADAYS

Remember my broken head, in the worship of the five
vowels!
NOUGHT   *generally in leg ∴ nothing!*

Yea, good sir, and the sciatica in my arm!
TITIVILLUS

I know full well what Mankind did to you;
Mischief hath informed me of all the matter through.   500
I shall venge your quarrel, I make God avow!
Forth, and espy where ye may do harm!
Take William Fide, if ye will have any mo.
I say, Newguise, whither art thou advised to go?

NEWGUISE

First I shall begin at Master Huntington of Sawston.   505
Fro thence I shall go to William Thurlay of Hauxton,
And so forth to Pichard of Trumpington—
I will keep me to these three.
NOWADAYS

I shall go to William Baker of Walton,
To Richard Bollman of Gayton.   510

---

493 *anon it be sought* let it be searched forthwith
494 *what ... aught* to see if you can steal anything
500 *me* ed (om MS)
503 *mo* more (companions)
504 *art thou advised* do you plan

---

497 *five vowels* Smart's suggestion (pp. 297–8) that there is an implied reference to
the 'five wells', a medieval term for the wounds of Christ, is attractive, but in
view of the many linguistic jokes in *Mankind* this is better seen as a case of
deliberate distortion, rather than scribal error.
498 *sciatica in my arm* The sciatic nerve affects the leg, so the supposed ailment is
comic nonsense.
503–16 The places and persons mentioned here are discussed in Smart, pp. 48–55
and 306–8. The location is near Cambridge, and most of the men can be
identified as people of local importance.

I shall spare Master Wood of Fulbourn—
He is a *noli me tangere*!

NOUGHT

I shall go to William Patrick of Massingham;
I shall spare Master Allington of Bottisham
And Hammond of Swaffham,   515
For dread of '*In manus tuas* ... queck!'
Fellows, come forth, and go we hence together.

NEWGUISE

Sith we shall go, let us be well ware whither.
If we may be take, we come no more hither;
Let us con well our neck-verse, that we have not a check.   520

TITIVILLUS

Go your way, a devil way, go your way all!
I bless you with my left hand: foul you befall!

516–17 *For ... together* ed (order of lines reversed in MS)
518 *ware* ed (ware & MS) careful
519 *take, we come* caught, we will come
520 *con* ed (com MS) memorize
520 *check* disaster
522 *foul you befall* a curse on you

---

512 *noli me tangere* 'touch me not', Christ's words to Mary Magdalene in the garden
after the Resurrection (John 20:17). In connection with a person the phrase
means 'an irascible fellow', and may be applied to Wood of Fulbourn for this
reason, or because he was a local justice and therefore a man to be avoided (see
Smart, pp. 49–51).

516 *In manus tuas* ... *queck* 'Into thy hands [I commend my spirit]', Christ's last
words (cf. Luke 23:46; also Psalms 30:6, AV 31:5, and *Everyman* 886). *The
Book of the Craft of Dying* (ed C. Horstman, *Yorkshire Writers* (London,
1895–96), II, p. 414) recommends that this be said by every Christian at the
point of death. *Queck*, here and in line 807, is the sound of strangulation by
hanging. For *In manus tuas* and *queck* in a hanging context see *Hick Scorner* 248
and *Youth* 101. Allington of Bottisham was to be avoided because he was a
Justice of the Peace; Hammond of Swaffham is not definitely known.

520 *neck-verse* 'A man might escape hanging for his first offence if he could read a
Latin verse, usually the third verse of the fiftieth Psalm ["Have mercy on me, O
God, according to thy great mercy. And according to the multitude of thy
tender mercies, blot out my iniquity (cf. AV 51:1)"] (Eccles). Cf. line 619 and
Hick Scorner 266: 'For we be clerks all and can our neck-verse'.

522 *I bless* ... *befall* The left hand is the devil's hand, and the 'blessing' is appro-
priately a curse. See M. Brown, *Left Handed: Right Handed* (Newton Abbot,
1979), pp. 39–43.

Come again, I warn, as soon as I you call,
And bring your advantage into this place.
                    [*Exeunt all but* TITIVILLUS]
To speak with Mankind I will tarry here this tide,   525
And assay his good purpose for to set aside.
The good man Mercy shall no longer be his guide.
I shall make him to dance another trace!

Ever I go invisible—it is my jet—
And before his eye thus I will hang my net,   530
To blench his sight. I hope to have his foot-met.
To irk him of his labour I shall make a frame:
This board shall be hid under the earth, privily.
                    [*Places a board in the earth*]
His spade shall enter, I hope, unreadily!
By then he hath assayed, he shall be very angry,   535
And lose his patience, pain of shame.
I shall meng his corn with drawk and with darnel;
It shall not be like to sow nor to sell.
Yonder he cometh! I pray of counsel.
He shall ween grace were wane.   540

[*Enter* MANKIND *with a bag of grain.* TITIVILLUS *is invisible to him*]

524 *And* ed (A MS)
524 *advantage* plunder, stolen goods
525 *tide* time
526 *assay . . . aside* try to corrupt his good intentions
529 *jet* fashion
531 *blench* deceive
532 *frame* scheme
534 *unreadily* with difficulty
535 *By then* By the time that
536 *pain of* on pain of
537 *meng* mix
537 *drawk . . . darnel* names of common weeds
538 *like* suitable
539 *of counsel* keep my secret
540 *ween grace were wane* believe he is without grace

531 *have his foot-met* (literally) have his foot-measure, cf. get the measure of him.

MANKIND

Now, God, of his mercy, send us of his sand!
I have brought seed here to sow with my land.
While I over-delve it, here it shall stand.
[Puts the bag down and prepares to dig. TITIVILLUS *steals it]*
In nomine Patris, et Filii, et Spiritus Sancti, now I will
    begin.
                    [The spade strikes against the board]
This land is so hard it maketh me unlusty and irk!   545
I shall sow my corn at a venture, and let God work.
                    [Looks for the bag]
Alas, my corn is lost! Here is a foul work!
I see well, by tilling little shall I win.

Here I give up my spade for now and for ever! *–bit rash + hasty!*
Here TITIVILLUS *goeth out with the spade [which* MANKIND
                                has thrown down]
To occupy my body I will not put me in dever;   550
I will hear my evensong here, ere I dissever.
This place I assign as for my kirk.
                    [Kneels and takes up his rosary]
Here, in my kirk, I kneel on my knees.
Pater noster, qui es in caelis ...

                    [Enter TITIVILLUS]

TITIVILLUS

I promise you, I have no lead on my heels! *[To the audience]*   555
I am here again to make this fellow irk.

541 *sand* bounty
542 *to sow with* with which to sow
543 *over-delve it* dig it over
544 *In ... Sancti* In the name of the Father, and of the Son, and of the Holy Spirit
545 *me* ed (om MS)
545 *unlusty and irk* weary and fed-up
546 *let God work* leave the outcome to God
550 *put me in dever* endeavour
551 *dissever* go
552 *kirk* church
554 *Pater ... caelis* Our Father, which art in heaven
555 *heels* ed (helys r.w. kneys, celis MS)

---

546 *at a venture* The MS reading *at wynter* makes no sense since the setting already
    is winter, or very early spring (cf. lines 54, 323, 332). Bevington's suggested
    emendation means 'at random', i.e. before the ground is properly prepared.
555 *lead on my heels* proverbial (cf. Tilley, L 136; Whiting, L 132).

Whist! Peace! I shall go to his ear and tittle therein.
'A short prayer thirleth heaven'.
 [*Talks in* MANKIND'S *ear*] Of thy prayer blin.
Thou art holier than ever was any of thy kin.
Arise and avent thee! Nature compels.   560
    [MANKIND *gets up, in obvious discomfort*]

MANKIND
 [*To the audience*] I will into the yard, sovereigns, and come
  again soon;
For dread of the colic, and eek of the stone,
I will go do that needs must be done.
    [*Throws down his rosary beads*]
My beads shall be here for whosomever will else. *Exiat*

TITIVILLUS
Mankind was busy in his prayer, yet I did him arise. 565
He is conveyed—by Christ!—from his divine service.
Whither is he, trow ye? Iwis—I am wonder wise—
I have sent him forth to shit leasings.
    [*Demonstrates one of his deceitful tricks*]
If ye have any silver—in hap pure brass—
Take a little powder-of-Paris, and cast over his face, 570
And even in the owl-flight let him pass.
Titivillus can learn you many pretty things!

557 *tittle* whisper
558 *blin* cease
560 *avent thee* relieve yourself
562 *stone* stone in the bladder
563 *that* that which
564 *for whosomever will else* no matter who wishes otherwise
564 *else* ed (cumme MS, but *ellys* where the line was written and cancelled after line
 561)
565 *did* made
568 *leasings* lies
572 *learn* teach

558 *A short prayer thirleth* [pierces] *heaven* traditional (cf. Smart, p. 299; Whiting,
 P357).
569–71 *If... pass.* If you have a 'silver' coin which is in reality only made of brass,
 sprinkle a little powder-of-Paris over its surface, and in the half-light you will
 be able to pass it off as silver. Titivillus may have 'demonstrated' this with some
 sort of conjuring trick. The exact composition of powder-of-Paris is not known,
 but Smart, p. 300, proposes an alchemical formula. For *owl-flight*, 'twilight',
 cf. *Magnificence* 671.

I trow Mankind will come again soon,
Or else, I fear me, evensong will be done.
His beads shall be triced aside, and that anon.   575
Ye shall a good sport if ye will abide.
Mankind cometh again! Well fare he!
I shall answer him *ad omnia quare*.
There shall be set abroach a clerical matter;
I hope of his purpose to set him aside.   580

[*Enter* MANKIND]

MANKIND
Evensong hath be in the saying, I trow, a fair while.
I am irk of it; it is too long by one mile.
Do way! I will no more so oft over the church stile;
Be as be may, I shall do another.
Of labour and prayer, I am near irk of both;   585
I will no more of it, though Mercy be wrath!
My head is very heavy, I tell you, forsooth.
I shall sleep full my belly, and he were my brother.
                                                     [*Sleeps*]

TITIVILLUS
And ever ye did, for me keep now your silence!
Not a word, I charge you!—pain of forty pence!   590
A pretty game shall be showed you, ere ye go hence.

575 *triced* flung
576 *shall* shall have
578 *ad omnia quare* to every question
579 *There ... matter* A subtle course of action shall be put into effect (literally
    'flowing')
581 *hath be in the saying* has been going on
584 *another* otherwise
586 *wrath* ed (wroth r.w. both, soth MS)
588 *I ... brother* I shall have a bellyful of sleep—I wouldn't care if he (Mercy) were
    my brother
589 *And* If
590 *pain of* on pain of forfeiting

Ye may hear him snore! He is sad asleep.
Whist! Peace! The devil is dead. I shall go round in his ear.
            [*Whispers to* MANKIND *in his sleep*]
Alas, Mankind, alas! Mercy has stolen a mare.
He is run away fro his master, there wot no man where.   595
Moreover, he stole both a horse and a neat.

But yet, I heard say he brake his neck as he rode in France;
But I think he rideth on the gallows, to learn for to dance,
Because of his theft; that is his governance.
Trust no more on him; he is a marred man.   600
Mickle sorrow with thy spade beforn thou hast wrought;
Arise, and ask mercy of Newguise, Nowadays, and
    Nought;
They can advise thee for the best; let their good will be
    sought.
And thy own wife brethel, and take thee a lemman.

[*To the audience*] Farewell, everychone! for I have done my   605
    game,
For I have brought Mankind to mischief and to shame!
    [*Exit*]

            [MANKIND *wakens*]

MANKIND
Whoop! Ho! Mercy has broken his neckercher, avows;
Or he hangeth by the neck, high upon the gallows!

592 *sad* soundly
593 *round* whisper
594 *has stolen* ed (stown MS)
596 *neat* cow
597 *as* ed (ab MS)
599 *governance* manner of behaviour
600 *marred* ruined
601 *beforn* previously
604 *brethel* abandon
604 *lemman* mistress
607 *neckercher* neckerchief (figuratively for 'neck')

---

593 *The devil is dead* a traditional saying meaning 'the job is almost done' (in this
    case, of winning Mankind to sin). See Smart, p. 300; *Oxford Proverbs*, p. 181;
    Tilley, D 244; Whiting, D 187.
607 *avows* it is said. Possibly read *a vows* and translate 'he says'.

Adieu, fair masters! I will haste me to the ale-house,
And speak with Newguise, Nowadays, and Nought, 610
And get me a lemman with a smattering face!

[*Enter* NEWGUISE *through the audience, breathless, with a
broken halter about his neck*]

NEWGUISE

Make space, for Cock's body sacred, make space!
Aha, well over-run! God give him evil grace!
We were near Saint Patrick's way, by him that me bought;

I was twitched by the neck; the game was begun; 615
A grace was, the halter brast asunder—*ecce signum!*
The half is about my neck. We had a near run!
'Beware', quod the good-wife, when she smote off her
husband's head, 'Beware!'
Mischief is a convict, for he could his neck-verse.
My body gave a swing, when I hung upon the case. 620
Alas he will hang such a likely man and a fierce
For stealing of an horse! I pray God give him care!

Do way this halter! What devil doth Mankind here, with
sorrow?
Alas, how my neck is sore, I make avow!

MANKIND

Ye be welcome, Newguise sir. What cheer with you? 625

NEWGUISE

Well, sir, I have no cause to mourn.

611 *And* ed (A MS)
616 *A ... signum* As luck would have it, the halter broke—behold the sign, proof
617 *near run* narrow escape
620 *case* gibbet
621 *Alas ... fierce* Alas that he (the executioner) should wish to hang such a
good-looking and fierce man
623 *Do way this halter* Off with this halter
623 *with sorrow* curse him

---

611 *smattering* flirtatious. Cf. *Magnificence* 1259, where *smatter* is glossed 'dabble
superficially'.
613 *over-run* out-run. Newguise is shouting back at the officer of the law, whom he
has outpaced.
618 *Beware ... Beware* The woman in the story gave her husband insufficient
warning, and the outcome was almost as disastrous for Newguise.
619 *Mischief...verse* Mischief has been tried and put in prison (rather than hanged)
because he knew (*could*) his neck-verse (cf. line 520n).

MANKIND
　　What was that about your neck, so God you amend?
NEWGUISE
　　In faith, Saint Audrey's holy band.
　　I have a little disease, as it please God to send,
　　With a running ringworm.   630

　　　　　[*Enter* NOWADAYS *with stolen church plate*]

NOWADAYS
　　Stand aroom, I pray thee, brother mine!
　　I have laboured all this night; when shall we go dine?
　　A church herebeside shall pay for ale, bread, and wine:
　　Lo, here is stuff will serve!
NEWGUISE
　　Now, by the holy Mary, thou art better merchant than I!   635

　　　　　　　[*Enter* NOUGHT]

NOUGHT
　　Avaunt, knaves, let me go by!
　　I cannot get, and I should starve!

　　[*Enter* MISCHIEF *with broken shackles fastened to him*]

MISCHIEF
　　Here cometh a man of arms! Why stand ye so still?
　　Of murder and manslaughter I have my belly-fill!
NOWADAYS
　　What, Mischief! Have ye been in prison? And it be your   640
　　　will,

627　*so God you amend* may God reform you (an asseveration)
634　*will serve* that will pay for it
636　*Avaunt* Out of my way
637　*I . . . starve* I cannot succeed in stealing, even if I should starve
640　*And* If

628　*Saint Audrey's holy band* 'A silk "lace" or necktie, much worn by women in the
　　　16th and early 17th c.' (*OED* s.v. *Tawdry Lace*). They probably commemo-
　　　rated the death of St Audrey from a tumour of the neck, which she considered
　　　just retribution for the fact that in the vanity of youth she had worn many
　　　splendid necklaces. Silk neckbands were hallowed at the saint's shrine in Ely
　　　cathedral (Eccles).
.638　*man of arms* Cf. 'knight of the collar', with reference to a hanged man, in *Youth*
　　　270.

Meseemeth ye have scoured a pair of fetters!
MISCHIEF
I was chained by the arms. Lo! I have them here.
The chains I brast asunder and killed the jailer,
Yea, and his fair wife halsed in a corner—
Ah, how sweetly I kissed the sweet mouth of hers!　　645

When I had do, I was mine own butler;
I brought away with me both dish and doubler.
Here is enow for me! Be of good cheer!
Yet well fare the new chesance!
MANKIND
I ask mercy of Newguise, Nowadays, and Nought;　　650
Once with my spade I remember that I fought;
I will make you amends, if I hurt you aught,
Or did any grievance.

NEWGUISE
What a devil liketh thee to be of this disposition?
MANKIND
I dreamt Mercy was hang—this was my vision—　　655
And that to you three I should have recourse and remotion.
Now, I pray you heartily of your good will;
I cry you mercy of all that I did amiss. [Kneels]
NOWADAYS
I say, Newguise, Nought; Titivillus made all this!
As sicker as God is in heaven, so it is.　　660

644 *halsed* embraced
646 *do* done
647 *doubler* plate
648 *enow* enough, plenty
649 *well ... chesance* here's to this new way of raising funds
654 *liketh thee* does it please you
656 *remotion* resort, recourse

641 *scoured a pair of fetters* Fetters were 'worn clean' by long use. Cf. Heywood, *The Pardoner and the Friar* (ed. J. S. Farmer, *The Dramatic Writings of John Heywood* (London, 1905), p. 24): 'thou shalt not escape me,/Till thous hast scoured a pair of stocks'. MS *scoryde* may have the secondary meaning 'scored, won by stealing' (Eric Partridge, *Dictionary of the Underworld* (London, 1961)), though this meaning is not recorded until much later.

NOUGHT

[*To* MANKIND] Stand up on your feet! Why stand ye so still?

NEWGUISE

Master Mischief, we will you exhort
Mankind's name in your book for to report.

MISCHIEF

I will not so: I will set a court,
And do it *sub forma juris*, dasard! 665

NOWADAYS   NOWADAYS *makes a proclamation*

Oyez, oyez, oyez! All manner of men and common women
To the court of Mischief either come or send!
Mankind shall return; he is one of our men. [*Sits*]

MISCHIEF

Nought, come forth. Thou shall be steward.

NEWGUISE

Master Mischief, his side-gown may be sold; 670
He may have a jacket thereof, and money told.

---

664 *set* convene
665 *And* ed (A MS)
665 *sub forma juris, dasard* in legal form, fool
666 s.d. NOWADAYS *makes a proclamation* ed (Nowadays mak proclamacyon MS)
666 *Oyez ... women* ed (written as two lines in MS)
667 *send* ed (sen MS, shortened for rhyme?)
669 *steward* recorder in a manor court
670 *side-gown* long gown of conventional cut
670 *sold* ed (tolde MS)

---

661 *Why stand ye so still?* probably meant sarcastically (Mankind is trembling like a leaf).
664 *court* The court of misrule, in which all decent values are reversed, calls to mind the similar one on the Boar's Head Tavern in Shakespeare's *1 Henry IV*, II.iv. Here the parody is of a manor court, with implications of the Last Judgment.
666 'Silence was called for by the usher or beadle, who then with his single "Oyez" if it were only a court for manorial business, or his triple "Oyez", if it were a leet court for graver business, commanded all those whose duty it was to be present to draw near' (H.S. Bennett, *Life on the English Manor* (Cambridge, 1937), p. 205). This and other references to the details of legal procedure suggest that the dramatist had some legal knowledge.
671 *and money told* with money to spare. Mankind's full and sober gown is to be cut down to make a dandy's jacket, leaving cloth which may be sold. Smart, pp. 304–5, quotes a statute of 1463 prohibiting any man from wearing 'gown, jacket, or coat, unless it be of such length that the same may cover his privy members and buttocks'.

MANKIND

I will do for the best, so I have no cold.
Hold, I pray you, and take it with you,
And let me have it again in any wise.
                    [*Takes off his gown*] NOUGHT *scribit*

NEWGUISE

I promit you a fresh jacket after the new guise.   675

MANKIND

Go and do that longeth to your office,
And spare that ye mow. [*Exit* NEWGUISE *with the gown*]

NOUGHT

Hold, Master Mischief, and read this.

MISCHIEF

[*Reads*] Here is '*Blottibus in blottis*
Blottorum blottibus istis'!   680
I beshrew your ears, a fair hand!

NOWADAYS

Yea, it is a good running fist;
Such an hand may not be missed.

NOUGHT

I should have done better, had I wist.

MISCHIEF

Take heed, sirs, it stands you on hand.   685

[*reads*] "*Curia tenta generalis,*
In a place there good ale is,
Anno regni regitalis
Edwardi nullateni,

672 *so* so long as
674 s.d. NOUGHT *scribit* NOUGHT writes
676 *that longeth* what is appropriate
677 *And* ed (A MS) ... *mow* And save what you can
682 *running fist* cursive hand
683 *may not be missed* should not be neglected (meant sarcastically)
684 *wist* known
685 *stands* ed (stonde MS) *you on hand* concerns you
686 *Curia* ed (Carici MS)

679–80 Doggerel Latin with no meaning.
686–92 The Latin ('a general court having been held, in the regnal year of Edward
the Nought ... in the regnal year of no king') is a bowdlerized version of the
opening formula of a manorial court record, perhaps alluding to the deposition
of Edward IV in 1470 (see the introduction, p. xiv). Mischief deflates the
pompous opening with a fatuous truism, that with the passing of February the
year comes completely to an end, 25 March being the start of the new year in the
middle ages.

On yestern day in Feverere ... the year passeth fully,   690
As Nought hath written—here is our Tully—
Anno regni regis nulli'.

NOWADAYS
What, ho, Newguise! Thou makest much tarrying.
That jacket shall not be worth a farthing.

[*Enter* NEWGUISE]

NEWGUISE
Out of my way, sirs, for dread of fighting!   695
Lo, here is a feat tail, light to leap about.
[*He displays* MANKIND'S *coat, much cut down*]
NOUGHT
It is not shapen worth a morsel of bread;
There is too much cloth; it weighs as any lead!
I shall go and mend it, else I will lose my head.
Make space, sirs, let me go out! [*Exit* NOUGHT *with the* 700
    jacket]

MISCHIEF
Mankind, come hither. God send you the gout!
Ye shall go to all the good fellows in the country about,
Unto the good-wife when the good-man is out:
'I will', say ye.
MANKIND   I will, sir.
NEWGUISE
There arn but six deadly sins—lechery is none,   705
As it may be verified by us brethels everychone.
Ye shall go rob, steal, and kill, as fast as ye may gone:
'I will', say ye.

693 *tarrying* ed (om MS)
695 *for dread of fighting* unless you want a fight
696 *feat ... about* neat cut, easy to move about in
699 *mend* alter
704 *I ... sir* ed (written as two lines in MS)
705 *arn but* are only
706 *brethels* villains
707 *gone* go

691 *Tully* Marcus Tullius Cicero, a model of Latin style and diction (said ironically
    of Nought, whose Latin is exceptionally poor).
695, 700 Apparently addressed to the audience.
702–3 Mischief now ritually charges Mankind to sin, starting with lechery.

MANKIND   I will, sir.

NOWADAYS
On Sundays, on the morrow early betime,
Ye shall with us to the ale-house early to go dine,   710
And forbear mass and matins, hours, and prime:
'I will', say ye.
MANKIND   I will, sir.

MISCHIEF
Ye must have by your side a long *da-pacem*,
As true men ride by the way for to unbrace them,
Take their money, cut their throats; thus overface them: 715
'I will', say ye.
MANKIND   I will, sir.

[*Enter* NOUGHT *with the jacket ridiculously abbreviated*]

NOUGHT
Here is a jolly jacket! How say ye?
NEWGUISE
It is a good jake-of-fence for a man's body!
                    [*They put it on* MANKIND *and chase him about*]
Hey, dog, hey! Whoop, whoo! Go your way lightly!
Ye are well made for to run!   720
MISCHIEF
Tidings, tidings! I have espied one!
Hence with your stuff! Fast we were gone!

709 *betime* in good time
711 *And* ed (A MS)
714 *unbrace* carve (as of poultry)
715 *overface* overcome
719 *lightly* quickly
720 *run* ed (ren r.w. amen MS)
721 *one* someone

---

711 *matins, hours, and prime* The seven canonical offices, or 'hours', sung daily in the
    monasteries <u>were</u> matins, prime, terce, sext, none, vespers, and compline.
713 *da-pacem* 'Nickname of a sword or dagger: Give-peace, Put-to-rest' (*MED*,
    citing only this example).
718 *jake-of-fence* protective jacket, properly one with metal plates inside the lining.
719 *Hey, dog, hey* Bevington suggest that in his new coat Mankind reminds New-
    guise of a racing dog.

are

I beshrew the last shall come to his home!
Dicant omnes
Amen!

[*Enter* MERCY]

MERCY
What ho, Mankind? Flee that fellowship, I you pray!   725
MANKIND
I shall speak with thee another time, tomorn or the next
      day.
We shall go forth together, to keep my father's year-day.
A tapster, a tapster! Stow, stat, stow!
MISCHIEF
Ah, mischief go with thee! Here I have a foul fall.
Hence, away fro me, or I shall beshit you all!   730
NEWGUISE
What ho! Ostler, ostler, lend us a football!
Whoop, how! Anow, anow, anow, anow! [*Exeunt all except*
      MERCY]

MERCY
My mind is dispersed; my body trembleth as the aspen
      leaf!

---

724 s.p. *Dicant omnes* Let all say
726 *thee* ed (om MS)
727 *my father's year-day* the anniversary of my father's death

---

723 *I beshrew ... home* Iona and Peter Opie, *Children's Games in Street and Play-
      ground*, p. 185, quote Samuel Rowlands (1600): 'Beshrow him that's last at
      yonder stile', and compare the present-day children's challenge: 'Last one there
      is a sissy!'
728 *Stow, stat, stow!* Here, woman, here! 'Stow' was a cry used in hunting and
      hawking.
729 *a foul fall* Mischief has taken a tumble in the confusion.
731 *Ostler ... football* The *ostler* could be either the keeper of the hostelry in which
      the play was performed, or a servant who attended the horses. The reference to
      football has been taken as a sign that *Mankind* was meant to be performed at
      Shrovetide, the period of three days immediately preceding Ash Wednesday,
      which was a time of feasting and hilarity when games of football were tra-
      ditionally played. See F. P. Magoun, *AHR* 35 (1929), 33–45; *HSN* 13 (1931),
      9–46.

The tears should trickle down by my cheeks, were not your
  reverence.
It were to me solace, the cruel visitation of death!   735
Without rude behaviour I cannot express this incon-
  —venience.
Weeping, sighing, and sobbing were my sufficience;
All natural nutriment to me as carrion is odible;
My inward affliction yieldeth me tedious unto your pres-
  ence.
I cannot bear it evenly that Mankind is so flexible.   740

E.E.Cummings.

Man unkind wherever thou be! For all this world was not
  apprehensible
To discharge thine original offence, thraldom, and captiv-
  ity,
Till God's own wellbeloved son was obedient and passible;
Every drop of his blood was shed to purge thine iniquity.
I discommend and disallow this often mutability;   745
To every creature thou art dispectuous and odible.
Why art thou so uncourteous, so inconsiderate? Alas, woe
  is me!
As the vane that turneth in the wind, so thou art convert-
  ible!

734 *were ... reverence* were it not out of consideration for you (the audience)
735 *were* would be
736 *cannot* ed (kan MS)
736 *inconvenience* misfortune
737 *sufficience* sustenance
738 *odible* hateful
739 *yieldeth me* makes me
740 *evenly* with equanimity
741–2 *apprehensible ... captivity* able to perceive how to atone for your original sin,
  bondage, and captivity (in the flesh)
743 *passible* able to suffer
745 *often* frequent
746 *dispectuous* despised
748 *convertible* changeable, fickle

742 *original offence* original sin, the innate human depravity inherited from Adam in
  consequence of the Fall.

In trust is treason; thy promise is not credible.
Thy perversious ingratitude I cannot rehearse.   750
To God and to all the holy court of heaven thou art
    despectible,
As a noble versifier maketh mention in this verse:
'*Lex et natura, Cristus et omnia jura*
Damnant ingratum; lugent eum fore natum'.

O good Lady and Mother of Mercy, have pity and compas- 755
    sion
Of the wretchedness of Mankind, that is so wanton and so
    frail!
Let Mercy exceed Justice, dear Mother! Admit this sup-
    plication,
Equity to be laid on party, and Mercy to prevail.

Too sensual living is reprovable that is nowadays,
As by the comprehence of this matter it may be specified.   760
Newguise, Nowadays, Nought, with their allectuous
    ways,
They have perverted Mankind, my sweet son—I have well
    espied.

Ah, with these cursed caitiffs, and I may, he shall not long
    endure!
I, Mercy, his father ghostly, will proceed forth and do my
    property.

749 *thy* ed (this MS)
750 *perversious* perverse
750 *rehearse* describe
751 *God and* ed (go on MS)
751 *despectible* contemptible
753 *et omnia* ed (sit omnia MS)
758 *on party* aside
761 *allectuous* enticing
763 *caitiffs* wretches
764 *property* natural office

---

749 *In trust is treason* proverbial (cf. Smart, p. 302); *Oxford Proverbs*, p. 842;
     Tilley, T 549; Whiting, T 492).
753–4 *Lex . . . natum* 'Law and nature, Christ and all justice condemn an ungrateful
     man, and lament that he was born'. The 'noble versifier' who composed this is
     unknown.
759–60 *Too . . . specified* Today's problems can be attributed to too sensual a way of
     life, as may be demonstrated by an understanding of the present situation.

Lady, help! This manner of living is a detestable pleasure.   765
Vanitas vanitatum! All is but a vanity!

Mercy shall never be convict of his uncourteous condition;
With weeping tears, by night and by day, I will go and
    never cease.
Shall I not find him? Yes, I hope. Now, God be my
    protection!
My predilect son, where be ye? Mankind, *ubi es*? [*Exit*]   770

[*Enter* MISCHIEF *and* NEWGUISE. *They shout after* MERCY]

MISCHIEF
My prepotent father, when ye sup, sup out your mess!
Ye are all to-gloried in your terms; ye make many a lease.
Will ye hear? He crieth ever 'Mankind, *ubi es*?'
NEWGUISE
Hic, hic, hic, hic, hic, hic, hic, hic!
That is to say: Here, here, here, nigh dead in the creek!   775
If ye will have him, go and seek, seek, seek!
Seek not overlong, for losing of your mind!

[*Enter* NOWADAYS *and* NOUGHT, *who urinate with their backs
to the audience*] → too far for audience now surely!

766 *Vanitas vanitatum* Vanity of vanities (Ecclesiastes 1:2)
770 *predilect* chosen
771 *prepotent* very powerful
772 *to-gloried* highfaluting
772 *lease* lie
774 *Hic* Here (Latin)
775 *nigh* ed (my MS)
777 *for* for fear of

---

767 *convict of his uncourteous condition* overcome by his (Mankind's) base nature, *or*
    found guilty of having an ungracious nature (referring to Mercy himself).
770 *ubi es?* where are you? Mercy's distressed search for Mankind recalls the parable
    of the good shepherd who searches for the lost sheep until it is found (Luke
    15:3–7).
771 *sup out your mess* sup up your drink (cf. line 269), nonsensically echoing
    Mercy's cries.
777 s.d. The bestiality of the vices, which is usually apparent from the defecatory
    references in their speech, is here taken a stage further. Nowadays seems, from
    lines 781–2, 784, to be urinating; Nought may be doing the same (line 785),
    though 'arrayed' in line 783 implies defecation (cf. Heywood, *Johan Johan*,
    256–7, ed. Bevington: 'And bicause it is aray'de at the skirt,/While ye do
    nothing, skrape off the dirt'). Nought may be the other side of a curtain and
    appear with his foot 'arrayed'.

NOWADAYS

[*To* MERCY] If ye will have Mankind—ho, *Domine, Domine,*
Dominus!—
Ye must speak to the shrive for a *cape corpus*,
Else ye must be fain to return with *non est inventus*!   780
[*To* NOUGHT] How say ye, sir? My bolt is shot.

NOUGHT

I am doing of my needings—beware how ye shoot!
Fie, fie, fie! I have foul arrayed my foot!
[*To the audience*] Be wise for shooting with your tackles,
for, God wot,
My foot is foully overshot!   785

MISCHIEF

A parliament, a parliament! Come forth—Nought,
behind!
A council, belive! I am afeard Mercy will him find.
How say ye? And what say ye? How shall we do with
Mankind?

NEWGUISE

Tish, a fly's wing! Will ye do well?
He weeneth Mercy were hung for stealing of a mare;   790
Mischief, go say to him that Mercy seeketh everywhere;
He will hang himself, I undertake, for fear.

MISCHIEF

I assent thereto; it is wittily said and well.

---

778 *Domine, Domine, Dominus* Lord, Lord, Lord
782 *needings* what is necessary
783 *arrayed* made a mess upon
784 *tackles* equipment, private parts
787 *belive* quickly
789 *a fly's wing* a trivial matter

779-80 *speak . . . inventus* Mercy must ask the sheriff for a *capias*, or writ of arrest, or
be satisfied with the reply that the defendant has not been found.
781 *My bolt is shot* The proverb runs: 'A fool's bolt is soon shot' (cf. *Oxford
Proverbs*, p. 276; Tilley, B 512, F 515; Whiting, B 434, F 408). In this case
Nowadays means that he has finished.
786 *Nought, behind* Nought may be kept in the background because of his soiled
foot.

NOWADAYS

Whip it in thy coat: anon it were done!
Now, Saint Gabriel's mother save the clouts of thy shoon!   795
All the books in the world, if they had be undone,
Could not 'a' counselled us bet. *Hic exit* MISCHIEF [*who returns with* MANKIND]

MISCHIEF

Ho, Mankind! Come and speak with Mercy; he is here fast by.

MANKIND

A rope, a rope, a rope! I am not worthy!

MISCHIEF

Anon, anon, anon! I have it here ready,   800
With a tree also, that I have get. [*They bring a gallows*]

Hold the tree, Nowadays! Nought, take heed, and be wise!
[NEWGUISE *demonstrates by putting his own head in the noose*]

NEWGUISE

Lo, Mankind! Do as I do; this is thy new guise.
Give the rope just to thy neck, this is mine advice.

[*Enter* MERCY *with a whip*]

MISCHIEF

Help thyself, Nought! Lo, Mercy is here!   805
He scareth us with a baleys; we may no longer tarry!
[*They run away.* NEWGUISE *nearly strangles himself with the rope*]

NEWGUISE

Queck, queck, queck! Alas, my throat! I beshrew you, marry!

796 *undone* opened (and perused)
797 *bet* better
797 s.d. *Hic* Here
801 *tree* gallows
804 *thy* ed (pye MS)
805 *Help* Save
806 *scareth us* is driving us off
806 *baleys* whip

794–5 *Whip* . . . *shoon* Apparently: 'If we quickly hand the problem over to you, it's as good as solved'. The extravagant blessing extends, if the emendation of MS *clothes* is correct, even to the pieces of metal with which Newguise's shoes are shod.
807 *Queck* the sound of choking (cf. line 516 and note).

Ah, Mercy, Christ's copped curse go with you, and Saint
    Davy!
Alas, my weasand! Ye were somewhat too near! *Exiant [all
    except* MERCY *and* MANKIND. MANKIND *throws himself on
                   the ground]*

MERCY

    Arise, my precious redempt son! Ye be to me full dear.   810
    [*Aside*] He is so timorous, meseemeth his vital spirit doth
      expire.

MANKIND

    Alas! I have be so bestially disposed I dare not appear;
    To see your solacious face I am not worthy to desire.

MERCY

    Your criminous complaint woundeth my heart as a lance.
    Dispose yourself meekly to ask mercy, and I will assent.   815
    Yield me neither gold nor treasure, but your humble
      obeisance,
    The voluntary subjection of your heart, and I am content.

MANKIND

    What! ask mercy yet once again? Alas, it were a vile peti-
      tion!
    Ever to offend and ever to ask mercy, it is a puerility.
    It is so abominable to rehearse my iterat transgression;   820
    I am not worthy to have mercy, by no possibility.

MERCY

    O Mankind, my singular solace, this is a lamentable
      excuse!

808 *copped* heaped-up
808 *Saint Davy* Saint David's
809 *weasand* throat
810 *redempt* redeemed
811 *is* ed (ys ys MS)
813 *solacious* comforting
814 *criminous complaint* guilty lament
819 *puerility* childish practice
820 *iterat* repeated

---

811 *vital spirit* According to medieval physiology, the three spirits which controlled
    the processes of life were the natural (located in the liver), the vital (in the
    heart), and the animal (in the brain).

The dolorous tears of my heart, how they begin to amount!
O pierced Jesu, help thou this sinful sinner to reduce!
Nam haec est mutatio dexterae Excelsi; vertit impios, et non   825
sunt.

Arise, and ask mercy, Mankind, and be associate to me.
Thy death shall be my heaviness. Alas, 'tis pity it should be
    thus!
Thy obstinacy will exclude thee fro the glorious per-
    petuity.
Yet, for my love, ope thy lips, and say '*Miserere mei, Deus!*'

MANKIND

The egal justice of God will not permit such a sinful wretch   830
To be revived and restored again—it were impossible!
MERCY
The justice of God will as I will, as himself doth preach:
Nolo mortem peccatoris, inquit, if he will be reducible.

MANKIND

Then, Mercy—good Mercy—what is a man without
    mercy?
Little is our part of paradise where mercy ne were.   835
Good Mercy, excuse the inevitable objection of my ghostly
    enemy.
The proverb saith, 'The truth trieth the self'. Alas, I have
    much care!

824 *pierced* ed (pirssie MS)
824 *this sinful sinner to reduce* to reform this sinner
828 *thee* ed (om MS)
828 *perpetuity* eternity
830 *egal* unbiased
832 *will as I will* desires what I desire
832 *preach* ed (precyse MS)
835 *where mercy ne were* if mercy should not exist
836 *objection* opposition

---

825 *Nam ... sunt* For this is the change of the right hand of the most High; he
    overthrows the wicked and they are no more (a combination of Psalms 76:11,
    AV 77:10, and an adaptation of Proverbs 12:7).
829 *Miserere mei, Deus* Have mercy on me, O God (the opening words of Psalms 50,
    55, 56, i.e. AV 51, 56, 57).
833 *Nolo ... reducible* I do not wish the death of the sinner, he said, if he can be
    converted (the sentiment and the Latin words are close to Ezechiel 33:11).
837 *The truth trieth the self* The truth is its own test. Whiting, T 514 cites only this
    instance, but cf. Carleton Brown (ed), *Religious Lyrics of the Fifteenth Century*
    (Oxford, 1939), p. 267: 'The trewth In dede hyt-selff well preffe'.

MERCY

God will not make you privy unto his Last Judgment.
Justice and Equity shall be fortified, I will not deny;
Truth may not so cruelly proceed in his strait argument 840
But that Mercy shall rule the matter without controversy.

Arise now, and go with me in this deambulatory;
Incline your capacity; my doctrine is convenient.
Sin not in hope of mercy; that is a crime notary.
To trust overmuch in a prince, it is not expedient. 845

In hope, when ye sin, ye think to have mercy, beware of
that adventure.
The good Lord said to the lecherous woman of Canaan—
The holy Gospel is the authority, as we read in scripture—
'Vade, et iam amplius noli peccare!'

Christ preserved this sinful woman taken in avowtry; 850
He said to her these words: 'Go, and sin no more!'
So to you: 'Go, and sin no more!' Beware of vain confi-
dence of mercy.
Offend not a prince on trust of his favour, as I said before.

If ye feel yourself trapped in the snare of your ghostly
enemy,
Ask mercy anon! Beware of the continuance! 855
While a wound is fresh, it is proved curable by surgery,
That, if it proceed overlong, it is cause of great grievance.

840 *strait* unyielding, strict
842 *deambulatory* covered walk
843 *Incline ... convenient* Try to understand; what I teach is to the point
843 *Incline ... convenient* ed (My doctrine ys conuenient Inclyne yowyr capacite
MS)
844 *notary* notorious
850 *avowtry* adultery
853 *I* ed (he MS)
855 *the continuance* continuing in sin

839–41 Justice, Truth, and Mercy are three of the daughters of God; the fourth is
Peace. These four debate the salvation of the Soul in *Perseverance*, 3129–3560.
The male sex of Mercy in *Mankind*, and of Truth in line 840, is unusual.
846 *In ... adventure* Beware of the risks of sinning in the hope of (subsequent)
mercy. For the sentiment see Ecclesiasticus 5:4–7.
849 *Vade ... peccare* Go, and now sin no more (John 8:11).

MANKIND

> To ask mercy and to have—this is a liberal possession!
> Shall this expeditious petition ever be allowed, as ye have
>   insight?

MERCY

> In this present life mercy is plenty, till death maketh his   860
>   division;
> But, when ye be go, *usque ad minimum quadrantem* ye shall
>   reckon your right.
>
> Ask mercy and have, while the body with the soul hath his
>   annexion;
> If ye tarry till your decease, ye may hap of your desire to
>   miss.
> Be repentant here; trust not the hour of death. Think on
>   this lesson:
> '*Ecce nunc tempus acceptabile, ecce nunc dies salutis*'.   865
>
> All the virtue in the world if ye might comprehend,
> Your merits were not premiable to the bliss above,
> Not to the least joy of heaven of your proper effort to
>   ascend;
> With mercy ye may—I tell you no fable; scripture doth
>   prove.

858 *liberal possession* generous gift to possess
859 *Shall ... insight?* Shall such a suddenly-made request ever be granted, from
       your understanding of the situation?
860 *plenty* plentiful
861 *go* dead
861 *shall* ed (scha MS)
862 *soul* ed (sowe MS)
862 *hath his annexion* is united
863 *hap of your desire to miss* chance to fall short of your wishes
867 *were not premiable to* would not merit

---

861 *usque ad minimum quadrantem* right to the last farthing. The language echoes
       Matthew 5 :26, and the theme recalls the struggle of Everyman to clear his book
       of accounts.
865 *Ecce ... salutis* Behold, now is the acceptable time; behold, now is the day of
       salvation (2 Corinthians 6 :2, which paraphrases Isaiah 49 :8).
866–9 The inevitability of sin means that man can only ever attain heaven through
       the grace of God, though his deeds influence the judgment which is passed on
       him. This is an important theme of the fourteenth-century poem *The Pearl*.

MANKIND

O Mercy, my suavious solace and singular recreatory, 870
My predilect special, ye are worthy to have my love!
For, without desert and means supplicatory,
Ye be compatient to my inexcusable reprove.

Ah, it sweameth my heart to think how unwisely I have
wrought!
Titivillus, that goeth invisible, hung his net before my eye, 875
And, by his fantastical visions seditiously sought,
To Newguise, Nowadays, Nought caused me to obey.

MERCY

Mankind, ye were oblivious of my doctrine monitory;
I said before, Titivillus would assay you a brunt.
Beware, fro henceforth, of his fables delusory! 880
The proverb saith, '*Jacula praestita minus laedunt*'.

Ye have three adversaries, and he is master of hem all,
That is to say, the Devil, the World, the Flesh and the Fell;
The Newguise, Nowadays, Nought, 'the World' we may
hem call,
And properly Titivillus signifieth the Fiend of hell; 885

The Flesh—that is the unclean concupiscence of your
body;

---

870 *suavious* pleasant
870 *singular recreatory* sole source of comfort
871 *predilect* chosen
872 *without ... supplicatory* though I am undeserving and without means of entreaty
873 *compatient* compassionate
873 *reprove* shame
874 *sweameth* grieves
876 *fantastical visions seditiously sought* illusory visions, seditiously contrived
878 *monitory* ed (manyterge MS) admonitory
879 *assay you a brunt* attempt an assault on you
881 *Jacula ... laedunt* Foreseen darts hurt less
882 *hem* them
883 *Fell* Skin
886 *concupiscence* lust

882–7 The idea is as old as St Augustine that the evil forces which assail man can be
grouped under the three main enemies, the World, the Flesh, and the Devil
(see S. Wenzel, *MS* 29 (1967), 47–66). In *Perseverance* Pride, Wrath, and
Envy are grouped with the devil, and Gluttony, Lechery, and Sloth are the sins
of the Flesh, while the World has as servants Lust and Liking and Folly.

These be your three ghostly enemies, in whom ye have put
    your confidence;
They brought you to Mischief, to conclude your temporal
    glory,
As it hath be showed before this worshipful audience.

Remember how ready I was to help you? Fro such I was   890
    not dangerous.
Wherefore, good son, abstain fro sin evermore after this!
Ye may both save and spill your soul, that is so precious.
Libere welle, libere nolle God may not deny, iwis.

Beware of Titivillus with his net, and of all his envious will,
Of your sinful delectation that grieveth your ghostly sub-   895
    stance.
Your body is your enemy; let him not have his will.
Take your leave when ye will. God send you good per-
    severance!

MANKIND
Sith I shall depart, bless me, father, here; then I go.
God send us plenty of his great mercy!
MERCY
Dominus custodit te ab omni malo   900
In nomine Patris, et Filii, et Spiritus Sancti. Amen.

                            Hic exit MANKIND

Worshipful sovereigns, I have do my property:
Mankind is delivered by my favoural patrociny;
God preserve him fro all wicked captivity,
And send him grace his sensual conditions to mortify!   905

Now, for his love that for us received his humanity,
Search your conditions with due examination.

890 *dangerous* aloof
892 *spill* destroy
893 *Libere welle, libere nolle* Freely to choose, freely to refuse
894 *his envious* ed (his Impyse *changed to* enmys MS)
895 *delectation* delight
903 *favoural patrociny* friendly patronage
906 *for ... humanity* for the love of him (Christ) who became man for our sake

---

900–1 *Dominus ... Sancti* 'The Lord keepeth thee from all evil' (Psalms 120:7, AV
    121:7). In the name of the Father, and of the Son, and of the Holy Spirit.

Think and remember the world is but a vanity,
As it is proved daily, by diverse transmutation.

Mankind is wretched; he hath sufficient proof;   910
Therefore, God grant you all *per suam misericordiam*
That ye may be play-feres with the angels above,
And have to your portion *vitam aeternam.* Amen!

Finis

909 *transmutation* changes
910 *he hath sufficient proof* he has been tested enough (cf. line 283)
910 *proof* ed (prowe r.w. abowe MS)
911 *grant* ed (om MS)
911 *per suam misericordiam* through his mercy
912 *play-feres* play-fellows
912 *angels* ed (angell MS)
913 *vitam aeternam* everlasting life

Key word summary

Mercy sermon
Mischief.
. . . .

N/N/N - dance, abuse →
Mankind intro
pleads to Mercy
N/N/N return to tempt Mankind →
Mercy gives last advice.
Mankind starts digging & N/N/N ←
                [Nowadays Nought through and.]

naughty song.
They mock Mankind & he beats them off with spade
                → + exits
→ Mischief. ←
        { N/N/N - complain to that they've been hit.
calls up Titivillus - audience must pay first
he sends them (N/N/N) out to do mischief
→ Mankind (only Tit. left - + he invisible)
(+ T. tricks him, - board on ground ∴ spade strikes it.
                    - mixes corn with weeds
                    - steals bag)
    prays - but T. whispers in ear!
            (magician trick)
M. fed up - sleeps
T. whispers that Mercy is hanged
Man wakes + wants to join N/W/N → exploits while a...
They enter + court of misrule to decide [jacket a...
+ they agree to join.

→ Mercy, but Mankind ex with N/N/N + Mischief.
    ↳ despairs + goes searching for man.

    NNN/Mis→ mock Mercy
        Now. + Nou. urinate on stage - turning pt.?
    . Mis. tells Man., Mercy looking for him
    (Man. attempts suicide.
    ↳ but Mercy enters with whip ∴ N/M/N/M →
    Mankind arrested
    Mercy forgives.

EVERYMAN

Here begynneth a treatyse how the
hye fader of heuen sendeth dethe
to somon euery creature to
come and gyue a counte
of theyr lyues in this
worlde and is in ma-
ner of a morall
playe.

Everyman.

Fig. 1. *Title-page of Everyman* [B]

DRAMATIS PERSONAE

MESSENGER
GOD
DEATH
EVERYMAN
FELLOWSHIP
KINDRED
COUSIN
GOODS
GOOD DEEDS
KNOWLEDGE
CONFESSION
BEAUTY
STRENGTH
DISCRETION
FIVE WITS, *the Five Senses*
ANGEL
DOCTOR

14 DISCRETION Soundness of Mind
15 FIVE WITS see *Mundus et Infans* line 883 and note
17 DOCTOR see the note on *Everyman* 902 s.p.

EVERYMAN

Here beginneth a treatise how the High Father of Heaven sendeth
death to summon every creature to come and give account of their
lives in this world, and is in manner of a moral play.

[*At one side of the acting area* GOODS, *concealed within a heap of boxes
and bags; at the other side* GOOD DEEDS, *fettered and weak on the
ground, which is strewn with the mutilated books of* EVERYMAN*'s deeds.
Enter* GOD, *in a high place, and* MESSENGER, *as prologue*]

MESSENGER
    I pray you all give your audience
    And hear this matter with reverence,
    By figure a moral play!
    The Summoning of Everyman called it is,
    That of our lives and ending shows   5
    How transitory we be all day.
    This matter is wondrous precious,
    But the intent of it is more gracious
    And sweet to bear away.
    The story saith: Man, in the beginning   10
    Look well, and take good heed to the ending,
    Be you never so gay!

---

3 *By figure* In form
6 *all day* always
7 *wondrous* ed (wonders A, wonderous B)

1s.p. MESSENGER The Prologue, spoken by the Messenger, is not in the Dutch
    original, *Elckerlijc*. Possibly it is by someone other than the main translator for it
    carelessly refers to characters (*Jollity* 16, *Pleasure* 17) who take no part in the
    play. In three other Moralities a Messenger has the same function as here, and
    several have a character simply called Prologue.
4 *The Summoning of Everyman* An abbreviation of this title (*The Som.*) is used as
    the signature-title in A; B has *The somonynge* (variously spelled); D has *Euery
    man.* C has no signature-title.
7–8 *This . . . gracious* The subject matter is of great value, but what it teaches is more
    full of divine grace.
10–11 *in the beginning . . . ending* For this proverb see *Mundus et Infans* 484 and note.

Ye think sin in the beginning full sweet,
Which in the end causeth the soul to weep,
When the body lieth in clay.   15
Here shall you see how Fellowship and Jollity,
Both Strength, Pleasure, and Beauty
Will fade from thee as flower in May;
For ye shall hear how our Heaven King
Calleth every man to a general reckoning.   20
Give audience, and hear what he doth say!

                                    [*Exit* MESSENGER]

GOD *speaketh*

GOD
I perceive, here in my majesty,
How that all creatures be to me unkind,
Living without dread in worldly prosperity.
Of ghostly sight the people be so blind;   25
Drowned in sin, they know me not for their God.
In worldly riches is all their mind;
They fear not my righteousness, the sharp rod.
My law, that I showed when I for them died,
They forget clean, and shedding of my blood red.   30
I hanged between two thieves, it cannot be denied;
To get them life I suffered to be dead.
I healed their feet; with thorns hurt was my head.
I could do no more than I did, truly.
And now I see the people do clean forsake me.   35
They use the seven deadly sins damnable,

---

23 *unkind* undutiful
25 *ghostly sight* spiritual vision
28 *rod* ed (rood A, rod B)
31 *thieves* ed (om A, theues B)

22–44 Speeches by God, lamenting man's sin and ingratitude, are known from the
Mystery Plays, such as the Towneley *Noah*.
33 *I healed . . . head* The allusion is to the occasion when Jesus *healed* (i.e. 'soothed,
comforted') the disciples' feet by washing them (John 13:1–20), in contrast to
his own treatment at the hands of man during the Passion. Alliteration accentu-
ates the contrast between *healed* and *hurt*.
36 *the seven deadly sins* The seven chief, or 'cardinal', sins entailing spiritual death
are pride, wrath, envy, sloth, gluttony, lechery, and covetousness (the *covetise* of
line 37). See M. W. Bloomfield, *The Seven Deadly Sins* (East Lansing, 1952) and
Mankind 882–7 and note.

As pride, covetise, wrath, and lechery
Now in the world be made commendable.
And thus they leave of angels the heavenly company.
Every man liveth so after his own pleasure,   40
And yet of their life they be nothing sure.
I see the more that I them forbear
The worse they be fro year to year.
All that liveth appaireth fast;
Therefore I will, in all the haste,   45
Have a reckoning of every man's person.
For, and I leave the people thus alone
In their life and wicked tempests,
Verily they will become much worse than beasts.
For now one would by envy another up eat;   50
Charity they do all clean forget.
I hoped well that every man
In my glory should make his mansion,

37 *As* With the result that
37 *covetise* covetousness, avarice
41 *nothing sure* not at all secure
42 *forbear* spare
43 *fro* from
44 *appaireth* deteriorates, decays
47 *and* if

---

40 etc. *Every man* The term Everyman/every man is variously printed in ABCD
with or without initial capital, and as either one or two words (with a strong
preference for two words in ACD and for one in B). God's speech is probably
deliberately ambivalent, for he is referring to the character in the play and to all
men, and his rebukes are therefore addressed partly to the audience. This
ambivalence explains the sudden shifts from singular to plural, especially in
lines 41–3, 52–4. The first unequivocal reference to the character Everyman is
in line 66, though Death speaks in general terms again until line 80.
46 *a reckoning* a receipt of account in the manner of an audit. See V. A. Kolve,
'*Everyman* and the parable of the Talents', pp. 316–40, and cf. *Mankind* 177,
Mundus et Infans 725–8.
49 *worse than beasts* cf. *Mankind* 165–6.
53 *mansion* permanent dwelling, natural resting place. Cf. Chaucer, *House of Fame*
751–5:
Hath fyssh duellynge in flood and see,
And trees eke in erthe bee.
Thus every thing, by thys reson,
Hath his propre mansyon,
To which hit seketh to repaire . . .

And thereto I had them all elect;
But now I see, like traitors deject,   55
They thank me not for the pleasure that I to them meant,
Nor yet for their being that I them have lent.
I proffered the people great multitude of mercy,
And few there be that asketh it heartily.
They be so cumbered with worldly riches   60
That needs on them I must do justice,
On every man living without fear.
Where art thou, Death, thou mighty messenger?

[*Enter* DEATH]

DEATH

Almighty God, I am here at your will,
Your commandment to fulfil.   65

GOD

Go thou to Everyman
And show him, in my name,
A pilgrimage he must on him take,
Which he in no wise may escape,
And that he bring with him a sure reckoning   70
Without delay or any tarrying.

DEATH

Lord, I will in the world go run over all
And cruelly outsearch both great and small.
Every man will I beset that liveth beastly,
Out of God's laws, and dreadeth not folly.   75
He that loveth richesse I will strike with my dart,
His sight to blind, and fro heaven to depart,

55 *deject* base
61 *needs* of necessity
73 *cruelly* unrelentingly, pitilessly
74 *beset* set about, attack
75 *Out of* At variance with
76 *richesse* wealth
77 *depart* separate

63 *Death, thou mighty messenger* In the N-Town *Death of Herod* Death introduces himself as 'Goddys masangere'.
68 *pilgrimage* The notion of life and death as a pilgrimage has its classic expression in Deguileville's fourteenth-century trilogy on the pilgrimage of human life, of the soul, and of Jesus. This was widely influential, and was the subject of several translations in verse and prose, one of which was printed by Caxton in 1483. Bunyan's *Pilgrim's Progress* belongs to the same tradition.

Except that Alms be his good friend,
In hell for to dwell, world without end.

[GOD *retires. Enter* EVERYMAN, *finely dressed*]

Lo, yonder I see Everyman walking;   80
Full little he thinketh on my coming.
His mind is on fleshly lusts and his treasure,
And great pain it shall cause him to endure
Before the Lord, Heaven King.
　　　　　　　　　[*Touches* EVERYMAN *with his dart*]
Everyman, stand still! Wither art thou going   85
Thus gaily? Hast thou thy maker forget?
EVERYMAN
Why askest thou?
Wouldest thou wit?
DEATH
Yea, sir, I will show you.
In great haste I am sent to thee   90
Fro God, out of his majesty.
EVERYMAN
What, sent to me?
DEATH
Yea, certainly.
Though thou have forget him here,
He thinketh on thee in the heavenly sphere,
As, ere we depart, thou shalt know.   95

---

88 *wit* ed (wete r.w. forgete A)

---

78 *Alms* By this passing reference to Alms (i.e. Good Deeds) the means of Everyman's salvation is suggested, even at this early stage.

84 s.d. *dart* Because of the uncertain meaning of Death's actions in *Everyman*, the
use of the dart is only conjectural though it is mentioned in line 76. Death is
shown striking Elckerlijc with a dart in the woodcut on the title-page of Vorsterman's edition of *Elckerlije*, (*c.* 1518–25), but not in the woodcuts in A and B
(see fig. 1). In Chaucer's *Pardoner's Tale* (*Canterbury Tales* C. 675–7) Death has
a spear with which he smites the heart (cf. *Everyman* 178).

85–6 *Everyman ... gaily?* Cf. Charity's word in *Youth* 476–7: 'Abide, fellow! a
word with thee./Whither go ye, tell me'.

95 *heavenly sphere* Medieval cosmologists believed that the universe was composed
of a series of concentric spheres with the earth at the centre. Beyond the sphere
of the earth was the sphere of the moon, then the spheres of the planets, then the
sphere of the fixed stars, then the *Primum Mobile* (the first moving thing, which
communicated its movement to everything else). Beyond that, God dwelt in an
unmoving heaven of pure light. See C. S. Lewis, *The Discarded Image* (Cambridge, 1964), pp. 92–121.

EVERYMAN

What desireth God of me?

DEATH

That shall I show thee.
A reckoning he will needs have,
Without any longer respite.   100

EVERYMAN

To give a reckoning longer leisure I crave.
This blind matter troubleth my wit.

DEATH

On thee thou must take a long journey;
Therefore thy book of count with thee thou bring,
For turn again thou cannot by no way.   105
And look thou be sure of thy reckoning,
For before God thou shalt answer and show
Thy many bad deeds, and good but a few,
How thou hast spent thy life, and in what wise,
Before the chief Lord of paradise.   110
Have ado that we were in that way,
For, wit thou well, thou shalt make none attorney.

EVERYMAN

Full unready I am such reckoning to give.
I know thee not. What messenger art thou?

DEATH

I am Death, that no man dreadeth,   115
For every man I rest, and no man spareth,

---

102 *This ... wit* I find this strange business disturbing
104 *book of count* book of account, list of good and bad deeds
105 *turn again* return
111 *ado that* ed (I do A, a do that B)
112 *make none attorney* appoint no one to take your place
115 *that no man dreadeth* that fears no one
116 *rest* arrest

---

111 *Have ado ... way* Have done, so that we can be on our way. Cawley changes *we* to *thou*, citing lines 141, 159 in support. But in line 130 Death commands 'Come hence', implying that, as in the Dance of Death in literature and art, he is going to accompany Everyman to the grave. Since Death gives Everyman a chance to make himself ready (line 181) and does not appear again (unless he does so silently at the grave), we seem to be left with a rather awkward blend of the traditional 'arrest' and an arrangement which gives Everyman the opportunity to reform. In *Perseverance* Humanum Genus also has just enough time to repent, despite the fact that Death has said (line 2840): 'Now I kylle the[e] ...'

For it is God's commandment
That all to me should be obedient.

EVERYMAN

O Death, thou comest when I had thee least in mind!
In thy power it lieth me to save.   120
Yet of my good will I give thee, if thou will be kind—
Yea, a thousand pound shalt thou have,
And defer this matter till another day.

DEATH

Everyman, it may not be, by no way.
I set not by gold, silver, nor richesse,   125
Ne by pope, emperor, king, duke, ne princess.
For, and I would receive gifts great,
All the world I might get.
But my custom is clean contrary.
I give thee no respite. Come hence, and not tarry.   130

EVERYMAN

Alas, shall I have no longer respite?
I may say, 'Death giveth no warning!'
To think on thee it maketh my heart sick,
For all unready is my book of reckoning.
But twelve year and I might have abiding,   135
My counting-book I would make so clear
That my reckoning I should not need to fear.
Wherefore, Death, I pray thee, for God's mercy,
Spare me till I be provided of remedy.

DEATH

Thee availeth not to cry, weep, and pray;   140
But haste thee lightly that thou were gone that journey,

---

125 *I set not* I am not influenced
135 *But ... abiding* If I might have respite for just twelve years
141 *lightly* quickly
141 *journey* ed (Iournaye r.w. praye A)

125–6 *I set not ... princess* The proverb says, 'Death takes high and low' (Whiting,
   D 101), but in the Dance of Death the rich still receive the most attention. In
   pictures, pope, emperor, king, queen, and cardinal are the most typical dancers
   (e.g. D. Briesemeister, *Bilder des Todes* (Unterschneidheim, 1970), fig. 77). In
   Lydgate's *The Daunce of Death* (ed F. Warren, *The Dance of Death* (London,
   EETS O.S. 181, 1931), pp. 6–22) the list begins pope, emperor, cardinal, and
   king, with baron and princess a little further behind.
132 *Death giveth no warning* proverbial. Whiting, D92, cites only this instance, but
   cf. *Hick Scorner* 930–2: 'Death ... giveth never no man warning'.

And prove thy friends if thou can,
For, wit thou well, the tide abideth no man,
And in the world each living creature
For Adam's sin must die of nature.   145

EVERYMAN

Death, if I should this pilgrimage take,
And my reckoning surely make,
Show me, for saint charity,
Should I not come again shortly?

DEATH

No, Everyman; and thou be once there,   150
Thou mayst never more come here,
Trust me verily.

EVERYMAN

O gracious God in the high seat celestial,
Have mercy on me in this most need!
Shall I have no company fro this vale terrestrial   155
Of mine acquaintance, that way me to lead?

DEATH

Yea, if any be so hardy
That would go with thee and bear thee company.
Hie thee that thou were gone to God's magnificence,
Thy reckoning to give before his presence.   160
What, weenest thou thy life is given thee?
And thy worldly goods also?

EVERYMAN

I had wend so, verily.

DEATH

Nay, nay, it was but lent thee.
For, as soon as thou art go,   165

---

142 *prove* test, make trial of
143 *tide* time
148 *saint* holy
159 *Hie thee* Hurry
161 *weenest* think
165 *go* dead

---

143 *the tide abideth no man* proverbial (cf. *Oxford Proverbs*, p. 821, which quotes
    Lydgate (*c.* 1440): 'The tid abit nat for no maner man'; Tilley, T 323; Whiting,
    T 318).
145 *of nature* By virtue of man's innate depravity, everyone must share in the
    mortality which is the consequence of Adam's fall.
161–70 Death reminds us here that he is no mere agent but a character in his own
    right serving the play's didactic purpose. Cf. Folly in *Mundus et Infans* 694–8.

Another a while shall have it, and then go therefro,
Even as thou hast done.
Everyman, thou art mad. Thou hast thy wits five
And here on earth will not amend thy life,
For suddenly I do come. 170

EVERYMAN

O wretched caitiff, whither shall I flee,
That I might scape this endless sorrow?
Now, gentle Death, spare me till tomorrow,
That I may amend me
With good advisement. 175

DEATH

Nay, thereto I will not consent,
Nor no man will I respite;
But to the heart suddenly I shall smite
Without any advisement.
And now out of thy sight I will me hie. 180
See thou make thee ready shortly,
For thou mayst say this is the day
That no man living may scape away. [*Exit* DEATH]

EVERYMAN

Alas, I may well weep with sighs deep!
Now have I no manner of company 185
To help me in my journey, and me to keep,
And also my writing is full unready.
How shall I do now for to excuse me?
I would to God I had never be get!

166 *go therefro* pass on
168 *wits* senses
169 *life* ed (lyue r.w. fyue A)
170 *For* In case
173 *gentle* noble, gracious
175 *advisement* deliberation, warning
186 *keep* protect
187 *my writing … unready* the preparation in writing of my list of good deeds io
    nowhere near ready
189 *be get* been born

---

166 *Another*. In *Perseverance* 2969–3007 Humanum Genus realizes his folly when
    he learns that his carefully-amassed wealth is to pass after his death to a servant
    of the World named I-Wot-Never-Who.
168 *Thou hast thy wits five* This reminder may seem rather odd here, as the
    character Five Wits does not appear until line 669. But the church's teaching
    was that the five senses, both inward and outward, could be put to either good
    or bad use (see *Jacob's Well*, pp. 216–27).
171 *wretched caitiff* poor wretch (Everyman's description of himself).
179 *Without any advisement* echoes *with good advisement* of line 175.

To my soul a full great profit it had be,   190
For now I fear pains huge and great.
The time passeth. Lord, help, that all wrought!
For though I mourn it availeth nought.
The day passeth and is almost ago.
I wot not well what for to do.   195
To whom were I best my complaint to make?
What and I to Fellowship thereof spake,
And showed him of this sudden chance?
For in him is all mine affiance.
We have in the world so many a day   200
Be good friends in sport and play.

[*Enter* FELLOWSHIP, *at a distance*]

I see him yonder, certainly!
I trust that he will bear me company;
Therefore to him will I speak to ease my sorrow.
Well met, good Fellowship, and good morrow!   205

FELLOWSHIP *speaketh*

FELLOWSHIP
Everyman, good morrow, by this day!
Sir, why lookest thou so piteously?
If anything be amiss, I pray thee me say,
That I may help to remedy.
EVERYMAN
Yea, good Fellowship, yea.   210
I am in great jeopardy.
FELLOWSHIP
My true friend, show to me your mind.
I will not forsake thee to my life's end,
In the way of good company.
EVERYMAN
That was well spoken, and lovingly.   215
FELLOWSHIP
Sir, I must needs know your heaviness;
I have pity to see you in any distress.
If any have you wronged, ye shall revenged be,
Though I on the ground be slain for thee,
Though that I know before that I should die.   220

199 *affiance* trust

EVERYMAN
Verily, Fellowship, gramercy.
FELLOWSHIP
Tush, by thy thanks I set not a straw!
Show me your grief, and say no more.
EVERYMAN
If I my heart should to you break,
And then you to turn your mind fro me   225
And would not me comfort when ye hear me speak,
Then should I ten times sorrier be.
FELLOWSHIP
Sir, I say as I will do, indeed!
EVERYMAN
Then be you a good friend at need!
I have found you true herebefore.   230
FELLOWSHIP
And so ye shall evermore,
For, in faith, and thou go to hell,
I will not forsake thee by the way.
EVERYMAN
Ye speak like a good friend; I believe you well.
I shall deserve it, and I may.   235
FELLOWSHIP
I speak of no deserving, by this day!
For he that will say, and nothing do,
Is not worthy with good company to go.
Therefore show me the grief of your mind,
As to your friend most loving and kind.   240
EVERYMAN
I shall show you how it is:
Commanded I am to go a journey,
A long way, hard and dangerous,
And give a strait count, without delay,
Before the high Judge, Adonai.   245

221 *gramercy* thank you
224 *break* reveal, open
235 *deserve* repay
242 *journey* ed (iournaye r.w. delaye A)
244 *strait count* precise account
245 *Adonai* Lord (a Hebrew word)

229 *a good friend at need* based on the proverb: 'A friend in need is a friend indeed'
(*Oxford Proverbs*, p. 289; Tilley, F 693; Whiting, F 634). Cf. line 854.

Wherefore, I pray you, bear me company,
As ye have promised, in this journey.

FELLOWSHIP

That is matter indeed! Promise is duty,
But, and I should take such a voyage on me,
I know it well it should be to my pain.　　　　　　　　250
Also it maketh me afeard, certain.
But let us take counsel here as well as we can,
For your words would fear a strong man.

EVERYMAN

Why, ye said if I had need
Ye would me never forsake, quick ne dead,　　　　　　255
Though it were to hell, truly!

FELLOWSHIP

So I said, certainly;
But such pleasures be set aside, the sooth to say;
And also, if we took such a journey,
When should we again come?　　　　　　　　260

EVERYMAN

Nay, never again, till the day of doom.

FELLOWSHIP

In faith, then will not I come there!
Who hath you these tidings brought?

EVERYMAN

Indeed, Death was with me here.

FELLOWSHIP

Now, by God that all hath bought,　　　　　　　　265
If Death were the messenger,
For no man that is living today
I will not go that loath journey!
Not for the father that begat me!

247 *journey* ed (iournaye r.w. adonay A)
251 *maketh* ed (make A, maketh B)
252 *take counsel* talk it over
253 *fear* frighten
255 *quick* alive
259 *journey* ed (iournaye r.w. saye A)
260 *again come* ed (come agayne A, cume agayne B)
265 *bought* redeemed
268 *loath* hateful
268 *journey* ed (iournaye r.w. to daye A)

248 *Promise is duty* a proverb, restated in its more familiar form in line 821:
'promise is debt'. Cf. *Oxford Proverbs*, p. 649; Tilley, P 603; Whiting, B 214.

EVERYMAN
Ye promised otherwise, pardie!   270
FELLOWSHIP
I wot well I said so, truly.
And yet, if thou wilt eat, and drink, and make good cheer,
Or haunt to women the lusty company,
I would not forsake you while the day is clear,
Trust me verily.   275
EVERYMAN
Yea, thereto ye would be ready!
To go to mirth, solace, and play
Your mind will sooner apply
Than to bear me company in my long journey.
FELLOWSHIP
Now, in good faith, I will not that way.   280
But, and thou will murder, or any man kill—
In that I will help thee with a good will.
EVERYMAN
O, that is a simple advice indeed!
Gentle fellow, help me in my necessity.
We have loved long, and now I need;   285
And now, gentle Fellowship, remember me.
FELLOWSHIP
Whether ye have loved me or no,
By Saint John, I will not with thee go.
EVERYMAN
Yet, I pray thee, take the labour and do so much for me
To bring me forward, for saint charity,   290
And comfort me till I come without the town.
FELLOWSHIP
Nay, and thou would give me a new gown,
I will not a foot with thee go;

---

270 *pardie* by God
271 *said* ed (say A, sayd B)
273 *haunt ... company* spend time in women's delightful company
274 *while the day is clear* while things go well
279 *journey* ed (iournaye r.w. waye A)
290 *bring me forward* accompany me

---

280 *will not* will not go, do not wish to go (a verb of motion is frequently omitted).
292 *give me a new gown* A fine gown was a sign of great affluence. Payments were
    sometimes made in this way, and an old gown was sometimes given as a gratuity
    (cf. *Paston Letters*, ed N. Davis (Oxford, 1971–76), II, p. 387).

But, and thou had tarried, I would not have left thee so.
And, as now, God speed thee in thy journey,   295
For from thee I will depart as fast as I may.

EVERYMAN

Whither away, Fellowship? Will thou forsake me?

FELLOWSHIP

Yea, by my fay! To God I betake thee.

EVERYMAN

Farewell, good Fellowship! for thee my heart is sore.
Adieu for ever! I shall see thee no more.   300

FELLOWSHIP

In faith, Everyman, farewell now at the ending.
For you I will remember that parting is mourning. [*Exit*
    FELLOWSHIP]

EVERYMAN

Alack! shall we thus depart indeed—
Ah, Lady, help!—without any more comfort?
Lo, Fellowship forsaketh me in my most need.   305
For help in this world whither shall I resort?
Fellowship herebefore with me would merry make,
And now little sorrow for me doth he take.
It is said, 'In prosperity men friends may find,
Which in adversity be full unkind'.   310
Now whither for succour shall I flee,
Sith that Fellowship hath forsaken me?
To my kinsmen I will, truly,
Praying them to help me in my necessity.
I believe that they will do so,   315

---

295 *journey* ed (Iournaye r.w. maye A)
298 *fay* faith
298 *betake* entrust
301 *ending* ed (ende AB)
303 *thus* ed (this A, thus B)
312 *Sith* Since

---

302 *parting is mourning* based on the proverb 'Sorrow is at parting if laughter be at
    meeting' (*Oxford Proverbs*, p. 754; Whiting, S 515). Cawley compares *Romeo
    and Juliet* II.ii.184: 'parting is such sweet sorrow'.
309–10 *In prosperity . . . unkind* No exact parallel for this proverb has been found,
    but *Oxford Proverbs*, p. 650, cites: 'In time of prosperity friends will be plenty;
    in time of adversity, not one amongst twenty' and 'Prosperity makes friends'.
    See also Tilley, T 301; and Whiting, P 417–18: 'In prosperity a man shall not
    know his friends'.

For 'Kind will creep where it may not go'.
I will go say, for yonder I see them.
Where be ye now, my friends and kinsmen?

[*Enter* KINDRED *and* COUSIN]

KINDRED

Here be we now at your commandment.
Cousin, I pray you show us your intent   320
In any wise, and not spare.

COUSIN

Yea, Everyman, and to us declare
If ye be disposed to go anywhither.
For, wit you well, we will live and die together.

KINDRED

In wealth and woe we will with you hold,   325
For over his kin a man may be bold.

EVERYMAN

Gramercy, my friends and kinsmen kind!
Now shall I show you the grief of my mind.
I was commanded by a messenger,
That is a high king's chief officer;   330
He bade me go a pilgrimage, to my pain,
And I know well I shall never come again.
Also I must give a reckoning strait,

317 *say* assay, try
317 *them* ed (them go ABD)
320-1 *show ... spare* tell us whatever is on your mind, and don't hold back
324 *we* ed (om A, we BD)
325-6 *we ... bold* we will stand by you, for a man can be confident of the support of
    his kinsmen
325 *hold* ed (bolde A, holde BD)
326 *bold* ed (holde A, bolde BD)

316 *Kind will creep where it may not go* Kinship, family ties will struggle on whatever
    the difficulties (crawl where it cannot walk). The same proverb is used with its
    original meaning, 'A man's true nature (kind) always asserts itself', in the
    Towneley *Second Shepherds' Pageant* 591-2. The meaning of *kind* seems to
    have been mistaken or deliberately adapted, for we also have 'Love will creep in
    service where it cannot go' (*Two Gentlemen of Verona* IV.ii.20). See *Oxford
    Proverbs*, p. 424. Whiting, K 36, cites 'Kind will have its course'.
320 *Cousin*. The term did not necessarily imply the same degree of kinship as it does
    today.

For I have a great enemy that hath me in wait,
Which intendeth me for to hinder.   335

KINDRED
What account is that which ye must render?
That would I know.

EVERYMAN
Of all my works I must show
How I have lived and my days spent;
Also of ill deeds that I have used   340
In my time, sith life was me lent,
And of all virtues that I have refused.
Therefore, I pray you, go thither with me
To help to make mine account, for saint charity.

COUSIN
What, to go thither? Is that the matter?   345
Nay, Everyman, I had liefer fast bread and water
All this five year and more!

EVERYMAN
Alas, that ever I was bore!
For now shall I never be merry,
If that you forsake me.   350

KINDRED
Ah, sir, what? Ye be a merry man!
Take good heart to you, and make no moan.
But one thing I warn you, by Saint Anne:
As for me, ye shall go alone.

EVERYMAN
My Cousin, will you not with me go?   355

COUSIN
No, by our Lady! I have the cramp in my toe.
Trust not to me, for, so God me speed,
I will deceive you in your most need.

---

346 *liefer* rather
348 *bore* born
357 *so God me speed* may God help me

---

334 *a great enemy that hath me in wait* a great enemy (the devil) who is on the lookout
for me (cf, *Mankind* 27, 40 etc., *Mundus et Infans* 751; and lines 599, 703, 883).
353 *Saint Anne* mother of the Virgin Mary
358 *I will ... need* This is the antithesis of what Knowledge says to Everyman in
lines 522–3. Cf. the World's promise in *Perseverance* 2698: 'In hys moste nede I
schal hym fayle'.

KINDRED

    It availeth not us to tice.

    Ye shall have my maid with all my heart; 360

    She loveth to go to feasts, there to be nice,

    And to dance, and abroad to start.

    I will give her leave to help you in that journey,

    If that you and she may agree.

EVERYMAN

    Now show me the very effect of your mind; 365

    Will you go with me or abide behind?

KINDRED

    Abide behind? Yea, that will I, and I may.

    Therefore farewell till another day! [*Exit* KINDRED]

EVERYMAN

    How should I be merry or glad?

    For fair promises men to me make, 370

    But when I have most need they me forsake.

    I am deceived; that maketh me sad.

COUSIN

    Cousin Everyman, farewell now!

    For, verily, I will not go with you.

    Also of mine own an unready reckoning 375

    I have to account; therefore I make tarrying.

    Now God keep thee, for now I go. [*Exit* COUSIN]

EVERYMAN

    Ah, Jesus, is all come hereto?

    Lo, fair words maketh fools fain.

    They promise and nothing will do, certain. 380

    My kinsmen promised me faithfully

    For to abide with me steadfastly,

    And now fast away do they flee;

    Even so Fellowship promised me.

    What friend were best me of to provide? 385

---

359 *It availeth ... tice* It's no use trying to entice us
361 *nice* wanton
362 *abroad to start* to gad about
365 *the very effect of your mind* your true intention
367 *and* if
378 *is all come hereto?* has everything come to this?
379 *fain* glad
385 *me of to provide* to provide myself with

---

379 *fair words maketh fools fain* proverbial (cf. *Oxford Proverbs*, p. 241; Tilley, W 794; Whiting, B 215).

I lose my time here longer to abide.
Yet in my mind a thing there is!
All my life I have loved riches;
If that my Good now help me might,
He would make my heart full light.   390
I will speak to him in this distress—
Where art thou, my Goods and richesse?

GOODS
Who calleth me? Everyman? What! hast thou haste?
I lie here in corners, trussed and piled so high,
And in chests I am locked so fast,   395
Also sacked in bags—thou mayst see with thine eye
I cannot stir—in packs low I lie.
What would ye have? Lightly me say.

EVERYMAN
Come hither, Good, in all the haste thou may,
For of counsel I must desire thee.   400

[GOODS *goes forward*]

GOODS
Sir, and ye in the world have sorrow or adversity,
That can I help you to remedy shortly.

EVERYMAN
It is another disease that grieveth me;
In this world it is not, I tell thee so.
I am sent for, another way to go,   405
To give a strait count general
Before the highest Jupiter of all.
And all my life I have had joy and pleasure in thee;
Therefore, I pray thee, go with me;
For, peradventure, thou mayst before God almighty   410
My reckoning help to clean and purify;
For it is said ever among
That 'Money maketh all right that is wrong'.

---

389 *Good* Goods, Property, Riches
403 *disease* problem, difficulty
410 *peradventure* perhaps
412 *ever among* commonly

---

413 *Money ... wrong* Whiting, M 630, cites a fourteenth-century version of this
proverb: 'Pecunia maket wrong rith, maket day niht, maket frend fo, maket
wele wo'. See also Tilley, M 1072–3.

GOODS

Nay, Everyman, I sing another song.
I follow no man in such voyages;   415
For, and I went with thee,
Thou shouldest fare much the worse for me;
For, because on me thou did set thy mind,
Thy reckoning I have made blotted and blind,
That thine account thou cannot make truly;   420
And that hast thou for the love of me.

EVERYMAN

That would grieve me full sore,
When I should come to that fearful answer.
Up, let us go thither together!

GOODS

Nay, not so! I am too brittle; I may not endure.   425
I will follow no man one foot, be ye sure.

EVERYMAN

Alas, I have thee loved, and had great pleasure
All my life-days on good and treasure.

GOODS

That is to thy damnation, without leasing,
For my love is contrary to the love everlasting.   430
But, if thou had me loved moderately during,
As to the poor give part of me,
Then shouldest thou not in this dolour be,
Nor in this great sorrow and care.

EVERYMAN

Lo, now was I deceived ere I was ware,   435
And all I may wite my spending of time.

GOODS

What, weenest thou that I am thine?

---

417 *shouldest* ed (sholdes A, shuldest BD)
419 *blind* illegible, difficult to read
420 *That* So that
421 *for the love of me* for having loved me
423 *answer* time of answering (before God)
426 *no* ed (om A, no BD)
429 *without leasing* without a lie
431 *during* during your life
433 *dolour* misery
435 *ware* aware
436 *all ... time* I can blame everything on having wasted my time

EVERYMAN

   I had wend so.

GOODS

   Nay, Everyman, I say no.

   As for a while I was lent thee;   440

   A season thou hast had me in prosperity.

   My condition is man's soul to kill;

   If I save one, a thousand I do spill.

   Weenest thou that I will follow thee?

   Nay, fro this world not, verily.   445

EVERYMAN

   I had wend otherwise.

GOODS

   Therefore to thy soul Good is a thief,

   For when thou art dead, this is my guise:

   Another to deceive in this same wise

   As I have done thee, and all to his soul's reprefe.   450

EVERYMAN

   O false Good, cursed thou be,

   Thou traitor to God, that hast deceived me

   And caught me in thy snare!

GOODS

   Marry, thou brought thyself in care,

   Whereof I am glad.   455

   I must needs laugh; I cannot be sad.

EVERYMAN

   Ah, Good, thou hast had long my heartly love!

   I gave thee that which should be the Lord's above.

   But wilt thou not go with me indeed?

   I pray thee truth to say.   460

GOODS

   No, so God me speed!

   Therefore farewell, and have good day! [*Exit* GOODS]

EVERYMAN

   O, to whom shall I make my moan

   For to go with me in that heavy journey?

   First Fellowship said he would with me gone;   465

442 *condition* nature, disposition
443 *spill* destroy
448 *guise* custom, practice
450 *reprefe* disgrace
453 *caught* ed (caugh A, caught BD)
457 *heartly* sincere
464 *journey* ed (iournaye r.w. gaye A)
465 *gone* go

His words were very pleasant and gay,
But afterward he left me alone.
Then spake I to my kinsmen, all in despair,
And also they gave me words fair;
They lacked no fair speaking,   470
But all forsake me in the ending.
Then went I to my Goods, that I loved best,
In hope to have comfort, but there had I least;
For my Goods sharply did me tell
That he bringeth many into hell.   475
Then of myself I was ashamed;
And so I am worthy to be blamed.
Thus may I well myself hate.
Of whom shall I now counsel take?
I think that I shall never speed   480
Till that I go to my Good Deed.
But, alas, she is so weak
That she can neither go nor speak.
Yet will I venture on her now.
My Good Deeds, where be you?   485

GOOD DEEDS

Here I lie; cold in the ground
Thy sins hath me sore bound,
That I cannot stir.

EVERYMAN

O Good Deeds, I stand in fear.
I must you pray of counsel,   490
For help now should come right well.

GOOD DEEDS

Everyman, I have understanding
That ye be summoned account to make
Before Messias, of Jerusalem King.
And you do by me, that journey with you will I take.   495

EVERYMAN

Therefore I come to you, my moan to make;
I pray you that ye will go with me.

---

469 *And* ed (An A, And BD)
483 *go* walk
488 *stir* ed (stere r.w. fere A)
491 *should come right well* would be very welcome
494 *Messias* Messiah
495 *And you do by me* If you follow my advice
496 *moan* lament

GOOD DEEDS

I would full fain, but I cannot stand, verily.

EVERYMAN

Why, is there anything on you fall?

GOOD DEEDS

Yea, sir, I may thank you of all.   500
If ye had perfectly cheered me,
Your book of count full ready had be.
[*Shows* EVERYMAN *his books of account*]
Look, the books of your works and deeds eke,
As how they lie under the feet,
To your soul's heaviness!   505

EVERYMAN

Our Lord Jesus help me,
For one letter here I cannot see!

GOOD DEEDS

Here is a blind reckoning in time of distress!

EVERYMAN

Good Deeds, I pray you help me in this need,
Or else I am for ever damned, indeed;   510
Therefore help me to make reckoning
Before the Redeemer of all thing,
That King is, and was, and ever shall.

GOOD DEEDS

Everyman, I am sorry of your fall,
And fain would I help you, and I were able.   515

EVERYMAN

Good Deeds, your counsel I pray you give me.

GOOD DEEDS

That shall I do verily:
Though that on my feet I may not go,
I have a sister that shall with you also,

499 *on you fall* happened to you
500 *of* for
503 *eke* also
505 *heaviness* grief
508 *Here* ed (There AB, Here D)

Called Knowledge, which shall with you abide,   520
To help you to make that dreadful reckoning.

. [*Enter* KNOWLEDGE]

KNOWLEDGE

Everyman, I will go with thee, and be thy guide,
In thy most need to go by thy side.

EVERYMAN

In good condition I am now in every thing,
And am wholly content with this good thing,   525
Thanked be God my creator!

GOOD DEEDS

And when she hath brought you there
Where thou shalt heal thee of thy smart,
Then go you with your reckoning and your Good Deeds
    together,
For to make you joyful at heart   530
Before the blessed Trinity.

EVERYMAN

My Good Deeds, gramercy!
I am well content, certainly,
With your words sweet.

KNOWLEDGE

Now go we together lovingly   535
To Confession, that cleansing river.

521 *dreadful* terrible, inspiring fear
525 *wholly* ed (hole A, holy BD)
526 *he* ed (by A, be BD)
527 *she* ed (he ABD)
528 *smart* suffering

---

520 *Knowledge* 'Self-knowledge' or 'acknowledgement of sin' are the usual inter-
pretations of the name, mainly on the evidence of the role the character plays in
preparing Everyman, going with him to Confession, and in helping him fulfil
his penance (see H. de Vocht, *Materialien* N.S. 20 (Louvain, 1947), pp.
59–64). Some have argued the more usual meaning of Knowledge (e.g. Kolve,
'*Everyman* and the Parable of the Talents', pp. 325–6). Cawley, pp. xxi–xxii,
shows that 'self-knowledge' and 'knowledge of God' were probably intended.
The name in *Elckerlijc, Kennisse*, means 'understanding', or simply 'Knowledge'.

EVERYMAN

For joy I weep! I would we were there!
But, I pray you, give me cognition
Where dwelleth that holy man, Confession.

KNOWLEDGE

In the House of Salvation—   540
We shall find him in that place,
That shall us comfort, by God's grace.

[CONFESSION *is seen at a distance within the House of Salva-*
tion. KNOWLEDGE *leads* EVERYMAN *there*]

Lo, this is Confession. Kneel down and ask mercy,
For he is in good conceit with God Almighty.

EVERYMAN

O glorious fountain, that all uncleanness doth clarify,   545
Wash fro me the spots of vice unclean,
That on me no sin may be seen.
I come with Knowledge for my redemption,
Redempt with heart and full contrition,
For I am commanded a pilgrimage to take,   550
And great accounts before God to make.
Now I pray you, Shrift, mother of salvation,
Help my Good Deeds, for my piteous exclamation!

538 *give me cognition* tell me, instruct me
544 *is in good conceit* has a good reputation
549 *Redempt with heart* Redeemed by earnestness
553 *for* in response to

---

540 *the House of Salvation* This is the only 'mansion' in the otherwise unlocalized
    action. Cawley, pp. xxix–xxx, suggests it might have been like the castle in
    Perseverance, for which an original stageplan survives; but it is difficult to
    envisage anything as substantial in the case of *Everyman*, which is on a much
    smaller and more intimate scale. Since it is the place of confession it would
    probably have resembled a church.
545ff Everyman's style of speech becomes more elevated as his spiritual condition
    improves.
549 *contrition* According to the religious treatise *Jacob's Well*, p. 167, the three parts
    of penance are contrition, confession, and satisfaction; and 'wyth thise thre
    instrumentys of penaunce, synne schal voyde, grace schal entre, and the
    kyngdam of heuene schal neyghin [draw near]'.
552 *Shrift* (i.e. Confession) is strangely referred to as feminine, in contrast with
    lines 539–44. Either this is a mistake or, as Cawley suggests, a more figurative
    sense may be intended here. *Confessio* in *Perseverance* is masculine throughout,
    and the equivalent in *Elckerlijc* is consistently feminine.

CONFESSION

I know your sorrow well, Everyman.
Because with Knowledge ye come to me,   555
I will you comfort as well as I can,
And a precious jewel I will give thee,
Called penance, voider of adversity.
Therewith shall your body chastised be,
With abstinence and perseverance in God's service.   560

[*Shows* EVERYMAN *the Scourge of Penance*]

Here shall you receive that scourge of me,
Which is penance strong that ye must endure,
To remember thy Saviour was scourged for thee
With sharp scourges, and suffered it patiently;
So must thou, ere thou scape that painful pilgrimage.   565
Knowledge, keep him in this voyage,
And by that time Good Deeds will be with thee.
But in any wise be sicker of mercy,
For your time draweth fast. And ye will saved be,
Ask God mercy, and he will grant truly.   570
When with the scourge of penance man doth him bind,
The oil of forgiveness then shall he find.

EVERYMAN

Thanked be God for his gracious work,
For now I will my penance begin.

---

558 *voider* ed (voyce voyder A, voyder BD) remover
565 *ere thou scape* before you escape
569 *draweth* draws near
569 *And* If
571 *him* himself

---

568 *sicker* certain. The form *seker* (AD) was understood in this sense by the editor
of B, who changed the word to *sure.* This meaning is preferred to the alternative
'seeker' because of the importance in the Moralities generally of the belief in the
constant availability of Mercy (cf. *Mundus et Infans* 850 and note). *Elckerlijc*
offers no clear guidance on this point.
572 *oil of forgiveness* J. Conley, *N&Q* N.S.22 (1975), 105–6, argues against Cawley's assertion that this is a reference to the oil used to anoint the dying in
Extreme Unction. He suggests that either the term is a metaphor for God's
mercy in general, or that it refers to the legend of the Oil of Mercy, which told
of Seth's attempts to procure the oil for his aged and ailing father, Adam.

This hath rejoiced and lighted my heart, 575
Though the knots be painful and hard within.

KNOWLEDGE

Everyman, look your penance that ye fulfil,
What pain that ever it to you be,
And Knowledge shall give you counsel at will
How your account ye shall make clearly. 580

EVERYMAN

O eternal God, O heavenly figure,
O way of righteousness, O goodly vision—
Which descended down in a virgin pure
Because he would every man redeem,
Which Adam forfeited by his disobedience— 585
O blessed godhead, elect and high divine,
Forgive my grievous offence!
Here I cry thee mercy in this presence.
O ghostly treasure, O ransomer and redeemer,
Of all the world hope and conduiter, 590
Mirror of joy, foundator of mercy,
Which enlumineth heaven and earth thereby,
Hear my clamorous complaint, though it late be;
Receive my prayers, unworthy in this heavy life.
Though I be a sinner most abominable, 595
Yet let my name be written in Moses' table!
O Mary, pray to the maker of all thing,
Me for to help at my ending,
And save me fro the power of my enemy,
For Death assaileth me strongly; 600

579 *at will* as you desire
586 *divine* divinity
588 *in this presence* before this company, audience
590 *conduiter* conductor, leader
591 *foundator* founder
592 *thereby* as a result (of all the qualities mentioned)

576 *Though ... within* i.e. the pain from the knots of the scourge will be hard to bear
inwardly (in the spirit) as well as outwardly (on the body).
585 *Which ... disobedience.* Either 'whom Adam caused to be damned by his
disobedience' (referring to *every man*) or 'whom Adam wronged' (referring to
God).
596 *Moses' table* The two tables, or tablets, of the law which Moses received on
Mount Sinai were taken to signify baptism and penance (de Vocht, op. cit., pp.
79–80).

And, Lady, that I may, by mean of thy prayer,
Of your son's glory to be partner,
By the means of his passion, I it crave.
I beseech you help my soul to save.
Knowledge, give me the scourge of penance;   605
My flesh therewith shall have acquaintance.
　　　[*He strips off his fine clothes and takes the scourge*]
I will now begin, if God give me grace.
KNOWLEDGE
Everyman, God give you time and space!
Thus I bequeath you in the hands of our Saviour.
Now may you make your reckoning sure.   610
EVERYMAN
In the name of the Holy Trinity,
My body sore punished shall be.
Take this, body, for the sin of the flesh!
　　　　　　　[*He scourges himself*]
Also, thou delightest to go gay and fresh,
And in the way of damnation thou did me bring;   615
Therefore suffer now strokes of punishing.
Now of penance I will wade the water clear,
To save me from purgatory, that sharp fire.
　　　　　　　[GOOD DEEDS *arises*]
GOOD DEEDS
I thank God! now I can walk and go,
And am delivered of my sickness and woe;   620

601–2 *I may . . . partner* through your intercession I may share in your son's glory
606 *have acquaintance* ed (gyue acqueyntaunce A, gyue a quytaunce B, haue aquain-
　　taunce D)
608 *space* opportunity
614 *gay and fresh* brightly and fashionably dressed (cf. *Mankind* 119)

---

618 *purgatory* 'Purgatory (Lat. *purgare*, to make clean, to purify) in accordance with
　　Catholic teaching is a place or condition of temporal punishment for those who,
　　departing this life in God's grace, are not entirely free from venial faults, or
　　have not fully paid the satisfaction due to their transgressions' (*Catholic Encyc-
　　lopedia*).
619 *now I can walk and go* 'According to Catholic doctrine, a man's good deeds have
　　no merit if he is guilty of unforgiven mortal sins, but revive and have merit
　　towards eternal bliss as soon as his sins are confessed and absolved' (Cawley).
　　Cawley goes on to quote Chaucer's *Parson's Tale* (*Canterbury Tales*, I.235):
　　'Thanne thilke goode werkes that been mortefied by ofte synnyng, whiche
　　goode werkes he dide whil he was in charitee, ne mowe nevere quyken agayn
　　withouten verray penitence'.

Therefore with Everyman I will go, and not spare.
His good works I will help him to declare.

KNOWLEDGE

Now, Everyman, be merry and glad!
Your Good Deeds cometh; now ye may not be sad.
Now is your Good Deeds whole and sound,   625
Going upright upon the ground.

EVERYMAN

My heart is light, and shall be evermore!
Now will I smite faster than I did before.

[He scourges himself again]

GOOD DEEDS

Everyman, pilgrim, my special friend,
Blessed be thou without end.   630
For thee is preparate the eternal glory.
Ye have me made whole and sound;
Therefore I will bide by thee in every stound.

EVERYMAN

Welcome, my Good Deeds! Now I hear thy voice,
I weep for very sweetness of love.   635

KNOWLEDGE

Be no more sad, but ever rejoice!
God seeth thy living in his throne above.

[KNOWLEDGE *gives* EVERYMAN *the Garment of Contrition*]

Put on this garment to thy behove,
Which is wet with your tears,
Or else before God you may it miss,   640
When ye to your journey's end come shall.

EVERYMAN

Gentle Knowledge, what do ye it call?

KNOWLEDGE

It is a garment of sorrow;
Fro pain it will you borrow;
Contrition it is,   645
That geteth forgiveness.
It pleaseth God passing well.

633 *in every stound* always
638 *behove* benefit
640 *Or ... miss* Or else you may feel the lack of it when you come before God
644 *borrow* protect
647 *It* ed (He AD, It B)

638 *Put on this garment* For the practice of changing garments to signify a change in
spiritual condition see *Mundus et Infans* 641–2n.

GOOD DEEDS

Everyman, will you wear it for your heal?

[EVERYMAN *puts on the garment*]

EVERYMAN

Now blessed be Jesu, Mary's son,
For now have I on true contrition;   650
And let us go now without tarrying.
Good Deeds, have we clear our reckoning

GOOD DEEDS

Yea, indeed, I have it here.

EVERYMAN

Then I trust we need not fear.
Now, friends, let us not part in twain.   655

KNOWLEDGE

Nay, Everyman, that will we not, certain.

GOOD DEEDS

Yet must thou lead with thee
Three persons of great might.

EVERYMAN

Who should they be?

GOOD DEEDS

Discretion and Strength they hight,   660
And thy Beauty may not abide behind.

KNOWLEDGE

Also ye must call to mind
Your Five Wits as for your counsellors.

GOOD DEEDS

You must have them ready at all hours.

EVERYMAN

How shall I get them hither?   665

KNOWLEDGE

You must call them all together,
And they will hear you incontinent.

EVERYMAN

My friends, come hither and be present,
Discretion, Strength, my Five Wits, and Beauty.

648 *heal* well-being, safety
653 *it* ed (om A, it B, them D)
656s.p. KNOWLEDGE ed (Kynrede AD, Kynred B)
660 *hight* are called
665 *hither* ed (hyder r.w. togyder A)
666s.p. KNOWLEDGE ed (Kynrede AD, Kynred B)
667 *incontinent* at once

[*Enter* DISCRETION, STRENGTH, FIVE WITS, *and* BEAUTY]

BEAUTY
Here at your will we be all ready; 670
What will ye that we should do?

GOOD DEEDS
That ye would with Everyman go,
And help him in his pilgrimage.
Advise you, will ye with him or not in that voyage?

STRENGTH
We will bring him all thither, 675
To his help and comfort, ye may believe me.

DISCRETION
So will we go with him all together.

EVERYMAN
Almighty God, lofed may thou be!
I give thee laud that I have hither brought
Strength, Discretion, Beauty, and Five Wits—lack I 680
    nought—
And my Good Deeds, with Knowledge clear;
All be in my company at my will here.
I desire no more to my business.

STRENGTH
And I, Strength, will by you stand in distress,
Though thou would in battle fight on the ground. 685

FIVE WITS
And though it were through the world round,
We will not depart, for sweet ne sour.

BEAUTY
No more will I, unto death's hour,
Whatsoever thereof befall.

DISCRETION
Everyman, advise you first of all; 690
Go with a good advisement and deliberation.
We all give you virtuous monition
That all shall be well.

674 *Advise you* Consider
678 *lofed* praised
678 *may* ed (myght A, may BD)
679 *laud* praise
687 *for sweet ne sour* come what may
688 *unto* until
692 *monition* warning

EVERYMAN

My friends, harken what I will tell—
I pray God reward you in his heavenly sphere—   695
Now harken, all that be here,
For I will make my testament
Here before you all present.
In alms half my good I will give with my hands twain
In the way of charity, with good intent,   700
And the other half still shall remain
In queth, to be returned there it ought to be.
This I do in despite of the fiend of hell,
To go quit out of his peril
Ever after and this day.   705

KNOWLEDGE

Everyman, harken what I say!
Go to Priesthood, I you advise,
And receive of him in any wise
The holy sacrament and ointment together;
Then shortly see ye turn again hither.   710
We will all abide you here.

FIVE WITS

Yea, Everyman, hie you that ye ready were.
There is no emperor, king, duke, ne baron,
That of God hath commission

695 *heavenly* ed (heuen A, heuenly BCD)
702 *there* to where
703 *despite* defiance
704 *quit* released
704 *peril* ed (perell r.w. hell A)
709 *together* ed (togyder r.w. hyder A)
714 *commission* authority

701–2 *remain/In queth* be set aside for restitution. *Jacob's Well* has much to say
   about restitution, which is the fourth part of satisfaction. Among the things
   which must be restored before the soul is completely cleansed are goods
   acquired by holy-day working, false oaths, false weights and measures, taking
   more than the service deserves, withholding wages, theft, false tithing, withholding debts, and simply having too much and giving too little to the poor
   (p. 196). In view of the inclusiveness of the requirement, no especially sinister
   crime need be imputed to Everyman.
709 *holy sacrament and ointment* the Viaticum (final Eucharist) and Extreme Unction (in which the dying man is anointed with ointment or oil).
713–68 The long sermon on priesthood, which is also in *Elckerlijc*, is seen by D. M.
   Bevington, *Tudor Drama and Politics*, pp. 35–7, as part of a contemporary
   general concern about the role of the clergy, and as a plea for reform.

As hath at least priest in the world being.   715
For of the blessed sacraments pure and benign
He beareth the keys, and thereof hath the cure
For man's redemption—it is ever sure—
Which God, for our soul's medicine,
Gave us out of his heart with great pain.   720
Here in this transitory life, for thee and me,
The blessed sacraments seven there be—
Baptism, confirmation, with priesthood good,
And the sacrament of God's precious flesh and blood,
Marriage, the holy extreme unction, and penance—   725
These seven be good to have in remembrance,
Gracious sacraments of high divinity.

EVERYMAN

Fain would I receive that holy body,
And meekly to my ghostly father I will go.

FIVE WITS

Everyman, that is the best that ye can do.   730
God will you to salvation bring,
For priesthood exceedeth all other thing.
To us holy scripture they do teach,
And converteth man from sin heaven to reach.
God hath to them more power given   735
Than to any angel that is in heaven.
With five words he may consecrate,— *Hoc est enim corpus meum*
God's body in flesh and blood to make,
And handleth his maker between his hands.
The priest bindeth and unbindeth all bands,   740
Both in earth and in heaven.

717 *cure* custody, responsibility
728 *Fain ... body* I would gladly partake of that holy body (in the form of the
    sacrament)

719–20 Cf. 751–3 By his death on the cross, Christ voluntarily gave to man his
    body and blood, which Catholics partake of in the Eucharist.
737 *five words* The five words with which the bread was consecrated were: *Hoc est
    enim corpus meum*, 'For this is my body'.
740–1 'Here "bind" and "unbind" are used in an ecclesiastical sense; cf. Matthew
    16:19, 18:18. Christ gave his apostles and their priestly successors the power to
    bind (retain) sins and, in the case of true repentance, to unbind (remit) sins.
    The priest, by withholding or granting absolution, decides what the sentence
    of a sinner shall be in this world and the next' (Cawley).

Thou ministers of all the sacraments seven,
Though we kiss thy feet, thou were worthy.
Thou art surgeon that cureth sin deadly.
No remedy we find under God   745
But all only priesthood.
Everyman, God gave priests that dignity,
And setteth them in his stead among us to be;
Thus be they above angels in degree.
[*Exit* EVERYMAN, *to receive the sacrament and extreme unction*
from the priest]

KNOWLEDGE

If priests be good, it is so, surely.   750
But when Jesu hanged on the cross with great smart,
There he gave out of his blessed heart
The same sacrament, in great torment.
He sold them not to us, that Lord omnipotent.
Therefore Saint Peter the apostle doth say   755
That Jesu's curse hath all they
Which God their Saviour do buy or sell,
Or they for any money do take or tell.
Sinful priests giveth the sinners example bad;
Their children sitteth by other men's fires, I have heard, 760
And some haunteth women's company
With unclean life, as lusts of lechery.
These be with sin made blind.

742 *of* ed (om ABD)
743 *thou were worthy* you would be worthy of it
747 *priests* ed (preest ACD, pryest B)
748 *stead* place
758 *tell* count, pay out

753 *same sacrament* Some editors emend to *seven sacraments* in line with *seven sacramenten* in *Elckerlijc*. But the reading in *Everyman* makes good sense, for it is specifically the body and blood of Christ which are referred to, which figuratively and literally issued from Christ's side on the cross. The lack of number concord with *them* (line 754) is of no consequence, as this is found elsewhere in *Everyman* (e.g. lines 40–1).
755–8 The allusion is to the sin of simony, the corrupt practice of buying or selling ecclesiastical preferments, or of traffic in sacred things. 'Any exchange of spiritual for temporal things is simoniacal' (*Catholic Encyclopedia*). The reference to St Peter is explained by Acts of the Apostles 8:18–24, which tells how the apostle rebuked a certain Simon for attempting to purchase with money the gift of the Holy Spirit.
760 An allusion to the illegitimate children of priests, implying the clergy's failure to observe the vows of chastity and celibacy.

FIVE WITS

I trust to God no such may we find;
Therefore let us priesthood honour,   765
And follow their doctrine for our souls' succour.
We be their sheep, and they shepherds be,
By whom we all be kept in surety.
Peace! for yonder I see Everyman come,
Which hath made true satisfaction.   770

GOOD DEEDS

Methink it is he, indeed.

[*Enter* EVERYMAN, *with a crucifix*]

EVERYMAN

Now Jesu be your alder speed!
I have received the sacrament for my redemption,
And then mine extreme unction.
Blessed be all they that counselled me to take it!   775
And now, friends, let us go without longer respite.
I thank God that ye have tarried so long.
Now set each of you on this rood your hand,
And shortly follow me.
I go before there I would be. God be our guide!   780
[*They grasp the crucifix in turn*]

STRENGTH

Everyman, we will not fro you go
Till ye have done this voyage long.

DISCRETION

I, Discretion, will bide by you also.

---

772 *your alder speed* the support of you all
778 *rood* ed (rodde ABCD)
780 *there I would be* to where I wish to be
780 *our* ed (your A, our BCD)

---

770 *satisfaction* See line 549n.
778 *rood* In view of the spelling *rodde* in ABCD, it is uncertain whether the intended
meaning is 'rood, cross', or 'rod, pilgrim's staff' (as suggested by F. A. Wood,
MP 8 (1910), 279). The meaning of the word in *Elckerlijc* is not clear. Cawley
shows that the author of the play *Homulus* (based on *Elckerlijc*) understood the
word to mean 'cross', and this sense seems preferable in *Everyman*. It was
presumably received from the priest who administered the last rites.

KNOWLEDGE

And though this pilgrimage be never so strong,
I will never part you fro.   785

STRENGTH

Everyman, I will be as sure by thee
As ever I did by Judas Maccabee.

[They journey to EVERYMAN*'s grave]*

EVERYMAN

Alas, I am so faint I may not stand!
My limbs under me doth fold.
Friends, let us not turn again to this land,   790
Not for all the world's gold,
For into this cave must I creep
And turn to earth, and there to sleep.

BEAUTY

What, into this grave? Alas!

EVERYMAN

Yea, there shall ye consume, more and less.   795

BEAUTY

And what, should I smother here?

EVERYMAN

Yea, by my faith, and never more appear.
In this world live no more we shall,
But in heaven before the highest Lord of all.

BEAUTY

I cross out all this! Adieu, by Saint John!   800
I take my tap in my lap, and am gone.

EVERYMAN

What, Beauty, whither will ye?

784 *strong* hard
786s.p. STRENGTH ed (lines 786–7 spoken by Knowledge ABC, by Strength D)
795 *consume, more and less* completely decompose
796 *smother* be suffocated

---

787 *Judas Maccabee.* Judas Maccabeus was a famous leader of the Jews in the second
century B.C. J. Conley, *N&Q* N.S.14 (1967), 50–1, suggests that this may be
an ironical allusion to the Nine Worthies, nine great heroes of antiquity
(including Judas Maccabeus) who became at death like all other men.

801 *I take my tap in my lap* 'To tak one's tap in one's lap, and sett aff. To truss up
one's baggage and be gone . . .; borrowed from the practice of those females,
who, being accustomed to spin from a rock [distaff], often carried their work
with them to the house of some neighbour. An individual, when about to
depart, was wont to wrap up, in her apron, the flax, or lint-tap, together with
her distaff' (*Jamieson's Dictionary of the Scottish Language*, under *Tap*).

BEAUTY

Peace! I am deaf; I look not behind me,
Not and thou wouldest give me all the gold in thy chest.

[*Exit* BEAUTY]

EVERYMAN

Alas, whereto may I trust?   805
Beauty goeth fast away fro me.
She promised with me to live and die.

STRENGTH

Everyman, I will thee also forsake and deny.
Thy game liketh me not at all.

EVERYMAN

Why, then, ye will forsake me all?   810
Sweet Strength, tarry a little space!

STRENGTH

Nay, sir, by the rood of grace!
I will hie me from thee fast,
Though thou weep till thy heart to-brast.

EVERYMAN

Ye would ever bide by me, ye said.   815

STRENGTH

Yea, I have you far enough conveyed.
Ye be old enough, I understand,
Your pilgrimage to take on hand.
I repent me that I hither came.

EVERYMAN

Strength, you to displease I am to blame;   820
Yet promise is debt—this ye well wot.

STRENGTH

In faith, I care not.
Thou art but a fool to complain.
You spend your speech and waste your brain.
Go thrust thee into the ground! [*Exit* STRENGTH]   825

EVERYMAN

I had wend surer I should you have found.
He that trusteth in his Strength

---

809 *liketh* pleases
814 *till* ed (to A, tyll BCD)
814 *to-brast* break to pieces
820 *you to displease* for displeasing you
821 *Yet ... wot* ed (Wyll ye breke promyse that is dette AC, Wyll you breke
     promyse/that is dette B, yet promise is dette/this ye well wot D)

She him deceiveth at the length.
Both Strength and Beauty forsaketh me,
Yet they promised me fair and lovingly.   830
DISCRETION
  Everyman, I will after Strength be gone;
  As for me, I will leave you alone.
EVERYMAN
  Why, Discretion, will ye forsake me?
DISCRETION
  Yea, in faith, I will go fro thee,
  For when Strength goeth before   835
  I follow after evermore.
EVERYMAN
  Yet, I pray thee, for the love of the Trinity,
  Look in my grave once piteously.
DISCRETION
  Nay, so nigh will I not come!
  Farewell, everychone! [*Exit* DISCRETION]   840
EVERYMAN
  O, all thing faileth, save God alone—
  Beauty, Strength, and Discretion—
  For when Death bloweth his blast
  They all run fro me full fast.
FIVE WITS
  Everyman, my leave now of thee I take;   845
  I will follow the other, for here I thee forsake.
EVERYMAN
  Alas, then may I wail and weep,
  For I took you for my best friend.
FIVE WITS
  I will no longer thee keep.
  Now farewell, and there an end. [*Exit* FIVE WITS]   850
EVERYMAN
  O Jesu, help! All hath forsaken me.

---

840 *everychone* everyone
849 *keep* attend

---

828 *She*. In *Pride of Life*, the earliest extant Morality Play, Strength is a knight, and promises to fight with Death. Strength in *Everyman* is feminine, and was probably more of an abstraction. Cf. also fig. 2, where strength is shown as male.
843 *when Death bloweth his blast* Death is often pictured with a trumpet or horn. See Briesemeister, *Bilder des Todes*, figs. 1, 3, 4, etc.

GOOD DEEDS

Nay, Everyman, I will bide with thee.
I will not forsake thee indeed.
Thou shalt find me a good friend at need.

EVERYMAN

Gramercy, Good Deeds! Now may I true friends see.   855
They have forsaken me, everychone.
I loved them better than my Good Deeds alone.
Knowledge, will ye forsake me also?

KNOWLEDGE

Yea, Everyman, when ye to death shall go;
But not yet, for no manner of danger.   860

EVERYMAN

Gramercy, Knowledge, with all my heart.

KNOWLEDGE

Nay, yet I will not from hence depart
Till I see where ye shall be come.

EVERYMAN

Methink, alas, that I must be gone,
To make my reckoning and my debts pay,   865
For I see my time is nigh spent away.
Take example, all ye that this do hear or see,
How they that I loved best do forsake me,
Except my Good Deeds that bideth truly.

GOOD DEEDS

All earthly things is but vanity—   870
Beauty, Strength, and Discretion do man forsake,
Foolish friends, and kinsmen, that fair spake—
All fleeth save Good Deeds, and that am I.

EVERYMAN

Have mercy on me, God most mighty,
And stand by me, thou mother and maid, holy Mary!   875

GOOD DEEDS

Fear not. I will speak for thee.

EVERYMAN

Here I cry God mercy!

---

868 *loved* ed (loue A, loued BCD)

867–9 *Take example ... truly* Even at this moment of crisis Everyman is made to
step outside the action and address the audience directly.

GOOD DEEDS
   Short our end, and minish our pain.
   Let us go and never come again.
EVERYMAN
   Into thy hands, Lord, my soul I commend!   880
   Receive it, Lord, that it be not lost!
   As thou me boughtest, so me defend,
   And save me from the fiend's boast,
   That I may appear with that blessed host
   That shall be saved at the day of doom.   885
   In manus tuas, of mights most
   For ever, *commendo spiritum meum.*
      [EVERYMAN *and* GOOD DEEDS *disappear into the grave*]
KNOWLEDGE
   Now hath he suffered that we all shall endure.
   The Good Deeds shall make all sure.

   [*Angelic music. An* ANGEL *appears in a high place with*
     EVERYMAN's *Book of Reckoning, and receives the soul, which
        has risen from the grave*]

   Now hath he made ending.   890
   Methinketh that I hear angels sing
   And make great joy and melody
   Where Everyman's soul received shall be.
ANGEL
   Come, excellent elect spouse, to Jesu!
   Hereabove thou shalt go   895
   Because of thy singular virtue.
   Now the soul is taken the body fro,

---

878 *Short ... pain* Shorten our time of death and diminish our pain
896 *singular* own, personal *or* exceptional

---

885 *day of doom* The Catholic doctrine of the particular judgment holds that
   immediately after death the eternal destiny of each separated soul is decided by
   the just judgment of God. In the general judgment on the day of doom all men,
   good and bad, will appear again to give a final account of their deeds.
886–7 *In manus ... meum* 'Into thy hands, most mighty one, I commend my spirit
   for ever', the last words spoken by Jesus on the cross (cf. Luke 23:46). For the
   significance of these words to the dying man see *Mankind* 516n.
894 *spouse* The soul as spouse of Christ is a common idea in medieval religious
   literature. If the ascent of the soul was actually shown, the player would
   probably have been a child, in keeping with iconographical conventions. In
   Perseverance 3578–9, God orders that the saved soul be brought to the scaffold
   representing heaven: 'Brynge hym to me / And set hym here be[by] my kne'.

Thy reckoning is crystal clear.
Now shalt thou into the heavenly sphere,
Unto the which all ye shall come   900
That liveth well before the day of doom.

[ANGEL *withdraws. Enter* DOCTOR, *as epilogue*]

DOCTOR
This moral men may have in mind.
Ye hearers, take it of worth, old and young.
And forsake Pride, for he deceiveth you in the end.
And remember Beauty, Five Wits, Strength, and   905
    Discretion—
They all at the last do every man forsake,
Save his Good Deeds there doth he take.
But beware! And they be small,
Before God he hath no help at all;
None excuse may be there for every man.   910
Alas, how shall he do then?
For after death amends may no man make,
For then Mercy and Pity doth him forsake.
If his reckoning be not clear when he doth come,
God will say, '*Ite, maledicti, in ignem aeternum*'.   915
And he that hath his account whole and sound,
High in heaven he shall be crowned—
Unto which place God bring us all thither,
That we may live body and soul together.
Thereto help the Trinity!   920
Amen, say ye, for saint charity! [*Exit*]

Finis

Thus endeth this moral play of Everyman, Imprinted in
    Paul's churchyard by me John Skot.

---

903 *take it of worth* take account of its merit
907 *Save ... take* But, on the contrary, he takes his Good Deeds there with him
911 *then* ed (than r.w. man A)

902s.p. DOCTOR The doctor as a specifically expository character is unparalleled
    among the Morality Plays, but appears in the Brome play of *Abraham and Isaac*,
    and elsewhere under different names. The equivalent in *Elckerlijc* is simply
    called Epilogue.
904 *Pride* Like Jollity and Pleasure (see line 1n), Pride has no role in the play.
915 *Ite...aeternum* Depart, you cursed, into everlasting fire (cf. Matthew 25:41).

Fig. 2. *Verso of Title-page of Everyman* [B]

APPENDIX

The Story of the Faithful Friend and its Exegesis in a Medieval Sermon[1]

I find a tale that there was sometime a man that had four friends. And in three of them specially he laid great affection in, but in the fourth he had but little affection in. So it befell on a time that he had trespassed against the king of the land, and so had forfeit against the law that he was worthy to die. And when that he was take [arrested] and should be brought to the doom [judgment], he prayed to them that took him that he might speak with his friends ere that he died.

He came to his first friend, that he trusted most in, and prayed him of his help and succour against the king. And this first friend answered him on this wise: 'The king's felon I will not hold nor maintain, for thou art worthy to die; and therefore rather I will buy thee a cloth to bury thee in'. Other answer he might none have. Then full sorrowfully he took his leave and went to assay his second friend, beseeching him of his help against the king, that he would grant him his life. And he answered him and said that the king's felon should have no other favour of him but that he would help himself to lead the king's traitor unto the death. Then when he might not speed [succeed] at the second, he went to assay the third friend, and came to him and prayed him that he would go with him and help him against the king, that he would forgive him his trespass. And he answered him and said that he would not help him, but, sith that [since] he was the king's traitor, he would help to hang him. Then he went to assay his fourth friend, the which he trusted least upon, and prayed him that he would go with him and pray for him to the king that he would forgive him his trespass. And then he answered him and said: 'Inasmuch as thou prayest me fair, though thou have but little deserved it, yet I will go with thee to the king and pray the king to forgive thee thy trespass; and rather than thou should be dead, I will die for thee myself'.

Now ghostly [devoutly] to speak to our purpose, the first friend that mankind seeketh most specially for help in need after his

---

[1] The story, which provides the plot of *Everyman*, is here adapted in a slightly modernized form from a sermon, probably of the late fourteenth century, edited in W. O. Ross, *Middle English Sermons* (London EETS O.S. 209, 1940), pp. 86–8. See p. 345 of the same edition for a concise summary of other versions.

death, it is the world. But what giveth the world to mankind after his death? In his life, I wot well, the world granteth to many men riches, mickle [great] pomp of the world, and many worships therewith. But what friendship showeth the world to mankind at the last end? Would thou see truly? Nought else but an old sheet to the earth to wrap him in. This is a lewd [worthless] friendship!

The second friend that mankind hath in this world, that is his father and his mother, his brether and his sustren [brothers and sisters], his wife and his children. But what friendship showeth these unto him? [They] weepen and cryen and wailen his death, and bringeth him to his grave, and there they leaven him; and after that the month mind[2] is do [done], anon after they have forget him ...

The third friend that cometh to mankind is the devil, to whom many men beeth inclined these days and beeth buxom[obedient] to his bidding, whatever that he biddeth them do. For there was never subject more buxomer to his prelate, nor wife to her husband, than many a man is to the devil. And anon as man is dead, the thief is ready to bring the soul into pain ...

Then sith that these three friends fail in the time of need, seek we then to the fourth friend, that is Christ, of the which friendship and love we may not be without, for his friendship delivers us from the bitter pains of hell, and restoreth us to everlasting life.

---

[2] *mind* 'The commemoration of a departed soul, esp. by a requiem said or sung on the day of the funeral in any month or year following' (*OED*).

MUNDUS ET INFANS

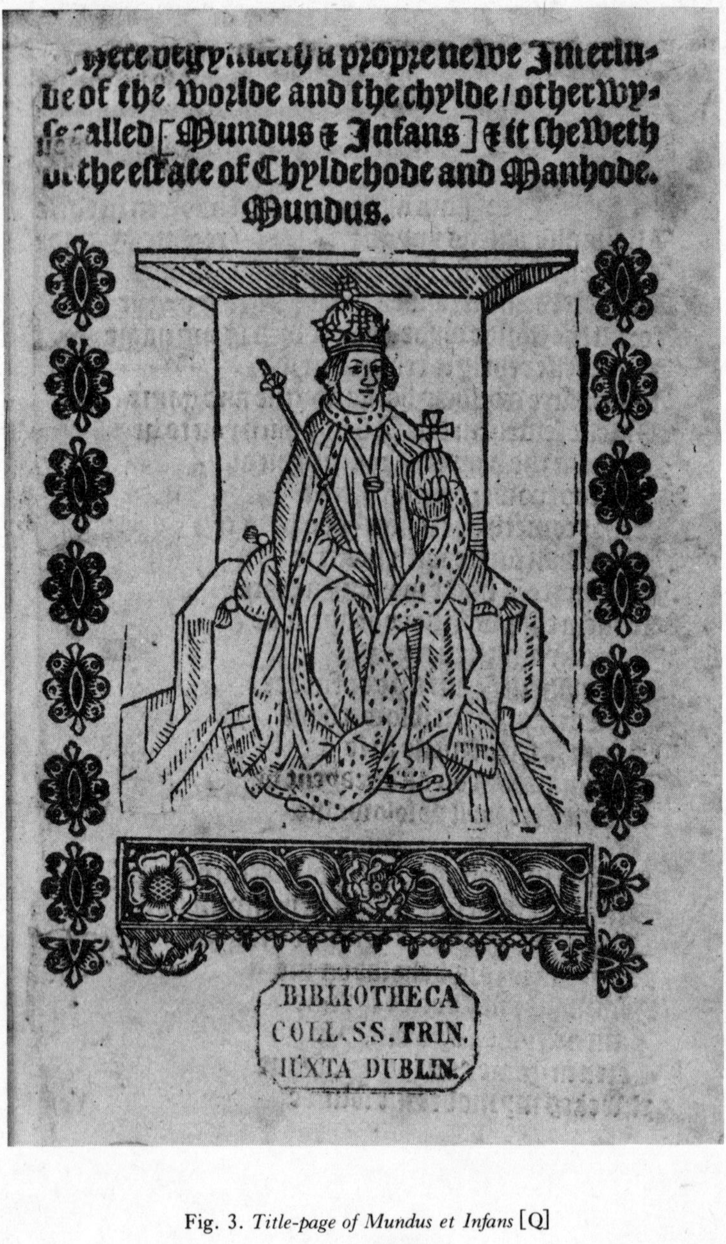

Fig. 3. *Title-page of Mundus et Infans* [Q]

DRAMATIS PERSONAE

MUNDUS, *the World*
INFANS, *the Child*
WANTON
LUST AND LIKING
MANHOOD
CONSCIENCE
FOLLY
PERSEVERANCE
AGE

MUNDUS ET INFANS

Here Beginneth a Proper New Interlude of the World and the
Child, Otherwise Called Mundus et Infans, and it Showeth of the
Estate of Childhood and Manhood.

[*Enter* MUNDUS]

MUNDUS

Sirs, cease of your saws, what so befall,
And look ye bow bonerly to my bidding!
For I am ruler of realms, I warn you all,
And over all foods I am king;

For I am king, and well known in these realms round;   5
I have also paleis i-pight,
I have steeds in stable, stalworth and strong,
Also streets and strands full strongly i-dight.

For all the World wide, I wot well, is my name.
All richesse redely it runneth in me,   10
All pleasure worldly, both mirth and game.
Myself, seemly in sale, I send with you to be,

For I am the World, I warn you all,
Prince of power and of plenty.
He that cometh not when I do him call   15
I shall him smite with poverty,

For poverty I part in many a place
To them that will not obedient be.

1 *saws* talk
2 *bonerly* meekly, courteously (i.e. bonairly, cf. debonair)
4 *foods* creatures
6 *paleis i-pight* established, built palaces
7 *stalworth* stalwart
8 *streets and strands* pathways and shores
8 *i-dight* manned
10 *All . . . me* All wealth certainly is found in me
12 *sale* hall, palace
17 *part* dispense

I am a king in every case;
Methinketh I am a god of grace;   20

    [Sits on his throne]

The flower of virtue followeth me.
Lo, here I sit seemly in see!
I command you all obedient be,
And with free will ye follow me.

    [Enter INFANS*]*

INFANS

[To the audience] Christ, our king, grant you clearly to
    know the case!   25
To move of this matter that is in my mind,
Clearly declare it, Christ grant me grace!

Now, seemly sirs, behold on me
How mankind doth begin:
I am a child, as you may see,   30
Gotten in game and in great sin.

Forty weeks my mother me found;
Flesh and blood my food was tho;
When I was ripe from her to found,
In peril of death we stood, both two.   35

Now to seek death I must begin,
For to pass that strait passage

---

19 *case* respect
22 *see* throne
25 *know the case* have good fortune
26 *move* speak
32 *found* maintained, bore, supported in her womb
33 *tho* then
34 *ripe from her to found* ready to depart from her (at birth)
37 *strait* narrow

23–4 *I command . . . me* The contradiction between obeying and exercising free will
may be intended as a sign of the extravagant irrationality typical of the boasting
speeches of Herod and other tyrants.
31 *Gotten . . . in great sin* Apocalypse 14 : 1–4 was the main authority for the belief in
the perfection of chastity. For a lively discussion of this see the prologue of *The
Wife of Bath's Tale* (*Canterbury Tales* D 1–162). The pain at childbirth was
linked to the idea of original sin by God's words to Eve: 'In sorrow shalt thou
bring forth children' (Genesis 3 :16).

For body and soul, that shall then twin
And make a parting of that marriage.

Forty weeks I was freely fed   40
Within my mother's possession;
Full oft of death she was adread,
When that I should part her from.

Now into the World she hath me sent,
Poor and naked—as ye may see;   45
I am not worthily wrapped nor went,
But poorly pricked in poverty.

Now into the World will I wend,
Some comfort of him for to crave.

             [*Approaches* MUNDUS]

All hail, comely crowned king!   50
God, that all made, you see and save!

MUNDUS
Welcome, fair child! What is thy name?
INFANS
I wot not, sir, withouten blame;
But oftime my mother in her game
Called me Dalliance.   55

46 *went* clothed
47 *poorly* ed (powerly Q)
47 *pricked* dressed
48 *wend* go
51 *see* protect
53 *withouten blame* with respect

38–9 The 'twinning', or separating, of body and soul is physically acted out in
    Perseverance 3007, when, as Humanum Genus dies, the soul crawls out from
    underneath the deathbed to plead for mercy. On soul as 'spouse' cf. *Everyman*
    894.
44–7 In *Nature*, p. 57, Man also arrives naked in the World's eyes. In answer to the
    World's offers he says:
    I thank you; but I need none other vesture;
    Nature hath clothed me as yet sufficiently.
    Guiltless of sin, and as a maiden pure,
    I wear on me the garment of innocency.
55 *Dalliance*, in relation to a child, means 'chatter', 'baby-talk', 'play'; but when he
    grows older it will imply 'amorous talk', 'flirtation'.

MUNDUS
> Dalliance, my sweet child!
> It is a name that is right wild,
> For when thou waxest old,
> It is a name of no substance.

> But, my fair child, what wouldest thou have?   60
INFANS
> Sir, of some comfort I you crave,
> Meat and cloth my life to save,
> And I your true servant shall be.
MUNDUS
> Now, fair child, I grant thee thine asking;
> I will thee find, while thou art ying,   65
> So thou wilt be obedient to my bidding.
> These garments gay I give to thee;

> *[Gives him clothes]*

> And also I give to thee a name,
> And clepe thee Wanton in every game,
> Till fourteen year be come and gone;   70
> And then come again to me.
WANTON
> Gramercy, World, for mine array,
> For now I purpose me to play.

57 *wild* imprudent, unreasonable
58 *waxest* grow
62 *Meat and cloth* Food and clothing
65 *ying* young
66 *So* On condition that
69 *clepe* call
72 *Gramercy* Thank you

---

63 *servant* Infans offers to become a retainer of the World in exchange for being
   accepted into his household and receiving livery from him, as from a temporal
   lord. For details of actual services and liveries see *The Household of Edward IV*,
   ed A. R. Myers (Manchester, 1959).
70 *fourteen year* Infans is at present seven years old (line 115), so seven years elapse
   in the course of the next fifty lines, and a further seven in the next thirty-five,
   including a span of two years between lines 144 and 155. Manhood also refers to
   a period of seven years in line 685. The seven-year periods are from the source
   poem, and do not reflect the actual periods of service in real life.

MUNDUS
 Farewell, fair child, and have good day.
 All recklessness is kind for thee.   75
                    [*Withdraws to his throne*]

WANTON
 Aha! Wanton is my name.
 I can many a quaint game.
 Lo, my top I drive, in same—
 See, it turneth round!
 I can, with my scourge-stick,   80
 My fellow upon the head hit,
 And wightly from him make a skip,
 And blear on him my tongue.

 If brother or sister do me chide,
 I will scratch and also bite;   85
 I can cry and also kick,
 And mock them all by row.
 If father or mother will me smite,
 I will wring with my lip,
 And lightly from him make a skip,   90
 And call my dame shrew.

 Aha! A new game have I found!
 See this gin? It runneth round.
 And here another have I found!
 And yet mo can I find.   95
 I can mow on a man,

75 *All ... thee* A completely carefree disposition is natural to you
77 *can* know
77 *quaint* clever
78 *in same* indeed (a rhyme tag)
80 *scourge-stick* stick of the whip used with the top
82 *wightly* nimbly
83 *blear ... tongue* stick out my tongue at him
87 *by row* ed (be rewe r.w. shrewe Q) one after another
89 *wring with* pucker
93 *gin* device, toy
95 *mo* more
96 *mow on* make faces at

---

75 s.d. Mundus probably does not go out either here or at line 130. His oversight of
    the intervening action is both allegorically apt and practically convenient.
76ff Wanton's speech gives the player the chance to enliven the part with various
    acrobatic antics. The visual focus (*Lo, See, here*, etc.) calls for demonstration or
    mime.

And make a leasing well I can,
And maintain it right well then—
This cunning came me of kind.

Yea, sirs, I can well geld a snail,   100
And catch a cow by the tail—
This is a fair cunning!
I can dance and also skip,
I can play at the cherry-pit,
And I can whistle you a fit,   105
Sirs, in a willow rine.

Yea, sirs, and every day,
When I to school shall take the way,
Some good-man's garden I will assay,
Pears and plums to pluck.   110
I can spy a sparrow's nest;
I will not go to school but when me list,
For there beginneth a sorry feast,
When the master should lift my dock.

But, sirs, when I was seven year of age,   115
I was sent to the World to take wage,
And this seven year I have been his page,
And kept his commandment.
Now I will wend to the World, the worthy emperor.

[*Goes to* MUNDUS]

97 *make a leasing* tell a lie
98 *then* ed (than r.w. man, can Q)
99 *cunning* knowledge, skill
99 *of kind* by nature
105 *fit* tune
109 *assay* test the quality of, sample
112 *but when me list* except when it pleases me
112 *list* ed (lest r.w. nest, fest Q)
114 *dock* 'The skirts or "tails" of clothes' (*OED*)

104 *the cherry-pit* 'A children's game which consists in throwing cherry-stones into a small pit or hole' (*OED*).
106 *willow rine* a musical pipe, possibly made by removing the pith of a green willow twig. *Rine* is probably *rind*, 'bark'.

Hail, lord of great honour! 120
This seven year I have served you in hall and in bower
With all my true intent.

MUNDUS

Now welcome, Wanton, my darling dear!
A new name I shall give thee here:
Love–Lust–Liking, in fere; 125
These thy names they shall be—
All game and glee and gladness,
All love-longing in lewdness.
This seven year forsake all sadness,
And then come again to me. 130

LUST AND LIKING

[*To the audience*] Aha! Now Lust and Liking is my name.
I am as fresh as flowers in May;
I am seemly shapen in same,
And proudly apparelled in garments gay;

My looks ben full lovely to a lady's eye, 135
And in love-longing my heart is sore set;
Might I find a food that were fair and free,
To lie in hell till doomsday for love I would not let
My love for to win.
All game and glee, 140
All mirth and melody,

125 *in fere* together
128 *lewdness* lasciviousness
133 *seemly shapen in same* very well-built
135 *ben* are
136 *sore* eagerly, exceedingly
137 *free* well-bred
138–9 *To ... win* I would not stop trying to win my loved one, even if I should lie in
hell till doomsday for it

125 *Love–Lust–Liking* means something like 'Passion and Pleasure in Love'. The
word *lust* was in the process of acquiring its pejorative connotations at this date,
but still required qualification if it were to imply 'lust' in the present-day sense.
A character called Lust and Liking, *alias* Voluptas, is servant of the World in
Perseverance.
132ff The diction and sentiments of this speech (*May ... love-longing ... fair and free
... love for to win*) are commonplace in medieval romances and secular lyrics.

All revel and riot,
And of boast will I never blin.

But, sirs, now I am nineteen winter old,
Iwis, I wax wonder bold.   145
Now I will go to the World
A higher science to assay.
For the World will me advance,
I will keep his governance,
For he is a king in all substance,   150
His pleasing will I pray.

[*Goes to* MUNDUS]

All hail, master full of might!
I have you served both day and night.
Now I comen, as I you behight.
One and twenty winter is comen and gone.   155
MUNDUS
Now welcome, Love—Lust and Liking!
For thou hast been obedient to my bidding,
I increase thee in all thing,
And mightily I make thee a man.

Manhood mighty shall be thy name.   160
Bear thee prest in every game,
And wait well that thou suffer no shame,
Neither for land nor for rent;
If any man would wait thee with blame,
Withstand him with thy whole intent;   165
Full sharply thou beat him to shame
With doughtiness of deed!

143 *blin* cease
145 *Iwis* Indeed
147 *science* knowledge, understanding
148 *For* Because
150–1 *For . . . pray* ed (lines in reverse order in Q)
154 *comen* come
154 *behight* promised
161 *Bear . . . game* Be prepared in every situation
162 *wait well* take care
163 *Neither . . . rent* i.e. Under no circumstances
164 *wait thee with blame* badly treat you
167 *doughtiness* bravery, toughness

For of one thing, Manhood, I warn thee:
I am most of bounty,
For seven kings suen me,   170
Both by day and night:
One of them is the king of Pride;
The king of Envy, doughty in deed;
The king of Wrath, that boldly will abide,
For mickle is his might;   175

The king of Covetise is the fourth;
The fifth king, he hight Sloth;
The king of Gluttony hath no jollity
There poverty is pight;
Lechery is the seventh king—   180
All men in him have great delighting,
Therefore worship him above all thing,
Manhood, with all thy might.

MANHOOD
Yes, sir king, without leasing,
It shall be wrought.   185
Had I knowing of the first king,
Well joyen I mote.

170 *suen* follow
175 *mickle* great
177 *hight* is called
179 *There poverty is pight* where poverty reigns
186 *king* ed (kynge without lesynge Q)
187 *joyen* rejoice
187 *mote* ed (mought Q) might

168–80 The traditional classification of sin under the three main Enemies of man
    gave the World a place alongside the Flesh and the Devil (see *Mankind* 882–7
    and note). According to the influential *Ancrene Riwle* (*c.* 1225), the World's sin
    is covetousness (Bloomfield, *The Seven Deadly Sins*, p. 149). In *Perseverance*
    the World does not have any of the deadly sins as servant, perhaps because
    Covetousness has his own scaffold and is his own master. Here in *Mundus et
    Infans* the tripartite division is suppressed, in keeping with the small scale of the
    play, just as the seven sins are subsumed in the one character Folly (see lines
    458–61).
176 *Covetise* Covetousness, Avarice. In Q this is spelled *couetous* in all instances but
    one (435 *couetys*), but this cannot have been the original spelling as *Covetise* is
    required for rhyme in lines 412, 441.

MUNDUS
The first king hight Pride.

MANHOOD
Ah, lord, with him fain would I bide.

MUNDUS
Yea, but wouldest thou serve him truly in every tide?   190

MANHOOD
Yea, sir, and thereto my troth I plight
That I shall truly Pride present;
I swear by Saint Thomas of Kent
To serve him truly is mine intent,
With main and all my might.   195

MUNDUS
Now, Manhood, I will array thee new
In robes royal right of good hue;

[*Revests* MANHOOD]

And I pray thee principally be true,
And here I dub thee a knight,
And haunt alway to chivalry.   200
I give thee grace and also beauty,
Gold and silver great plenty,
Of the wrong to make the right.

189 *fain* gladly
190 *in every tide* at all times
192 *present* present myself to
200 *haunt alway* always practise, use

---

193 *Saint Thomas of Kent* Thomas Becket, martyred in Canterbury Cathedral in
1170, the principal English saint in the middle ages.
199–203 *dub thee a knight … right* In the fifteenth-century ceremony for making
Knights of the Bath, the squire at his creation swore to love God, sustain the
church, and support the sovereign; also to be discrete, true to promise, and
just, and to support widows and maidens with money, 'that for lak of good they
be not mysgovernyd' (see Viscount Dillon, *Archaeologia* 57 (1900), 67–8). The
last promise explains line 203, though there is an ominous echo of the proverb
'Money maketh all right that is wrong', the belief which led Everyman astray
(cf. *Everyman* 413).

MANHOOD

   Gramercy, World and emperor!
   Gramercy, World and governor!   205
   Gramercy, comfort in all colour!
   And now I take my leave. Farewell!

MUNDUS

   Farewell, Manhood, my gentle knight!
   Farewell, my son, seemly in sight!
   I give thee a sword, and also strength and might,   210
   In battle boldly to bear thee well.

MANHOOD

   Now I am dubbed a knight hend,
   Wonder wide shall wax my fame.
   To seek adventures now will I wend,
   To please the World in glee and game.   215

MUNDUS

   Lo, sirs, I am a prince perilous i-proved,
   I-proved full perilous and pithily i-pight.
   As a lord in each land I am beloved.
   Mine eyen do shine as lantern bright.

   I am a creature comely, out of care.   220
   Emperors and kings they kneel to my knee;
   Every man is afeard when I do on him stare,
   For all merry middle-earth maketh mention of me.

   Yet all is at my handwork, both by down and by dale,
   Both the sea and the land, and fowls that fly.   225

206 *in all colour* in every respect
208 *gentle* noble
209 *seemly in sight* good-looking
212 *hend* gallant
215 *glee and game* merriment and pleasure
217 *pithily i-pight* firmly established
219 *eyen* eyes
220 *out of care* without doubt
223 *middle-earth* the earth, as opposed to heaven (above) and hell (below)
224 *Yet ... dale* Everything everywhere is under my control

224–7 *Yet all ... sky* The World's hyperbole spills over into blasphemy, for these
    are the works of God and recall the Creation. The proud boasts suggest those of
    Lucifer, the angel bright as the morning star, who aspired to be equal to God
    and was cast into hell for his presumption.

And I were once moved, I tell you in tale,
There durst no star stir that standeth in the sky;

For I am lord and leader, so that in land
All boweth to my bidding bonerly about.
Who that stirreth with any strife or waiteth me with wrong,   230
I shall mightily make him to stammer and stoop,
For I am richest in mine array;
I have knights and towers,
I have ladies brightest in bowers.
Now will I fare on these flowers.   235
Lordings, have good day!   [*Exit* MUNDUS]

MANHOOD
Peace, now peace, ye fellows all about,
Peace now, and harken to my saws!
For I am lord both stalworthy and stout;
All lands are led by my laws.   240

Baron was there never born that so well him bore,
A better ne a bolder nor a brighter of blee,
For I have might and main over countries far,
And Manhood mighty am I named in every country.

226 *And ... tale* Should I be angered, I assure you
230 *waiteth me with wrong* lies in wait for me
239 *stalworthy* stalwart
241 *bore* ed (bare r.w. fare Q)
242 *bolder* ed (bolde Q)
242 *blee* countenance

---

235 *fare on these flowers* go to meet these delightful creatures (the ladies). Lancashire, p. 96, takes Q's *flourys* to mean 'floors'.
237ff Manhood, now that he has come of age, exhibits all the pride and wrath that
has hitherto been characteristic of the World. This is probably meant to signify
that Manhood is now fully initiated into the ways of the World, a point which is
underscored when he sits on the World's throne at line 287. In *Nature*, p. 81,
Man becomes acquainted with the seven deadly sins, who have changed their
names in order to deceive him. Of these 'Wrath, because he is somewhat
hasty,/Is called Manhood'.

For Salerno and Samers, and Inde the Lois,   245
Calais, Kent, and Cornwall I have conquered clean,
Picardy, and Pontoise, and gentle Artois,
Florence, Flanders, and France, and also Gascoigne—
All I have conquered as a knight.
There is no emperor so keen,   250
That dare me lightly teen,
For lives and limbs I lean,
So mickle is my might.

For I have boldly blood full piteously dispilled,
There many have left fingers and feet, both head and face.   255
I have done harm on heads, and knights have I killed,
And many a lady for my love hath said 'Alas!'

Brigand harness I have beaten to back and to bones,
And beaten also many a groom to ground;
Breastplates I have beaten, as Stephen was with stones,   260

---

246 *clean* absolutely
251 *teen* vex
252 *lean* weaken, diminish
255 *There* where
257 *for my love* for love of me
259 *groom* man

245–9 *Salerno ... knight* The places names are in England, France, Italy, and the
     Middle East. *Inde the Lois* (ynde the loys Q) is 'India the Less', a name which
     Caxton used in 1480 to signify Asia Minor (see O. H. Prior (ed), *Caxton's
     Mirrour of the World* (London, EETS E.S. 110, 1913), p. 85). Sugden, p. 291,
     sees in line 246 a reference to the victory of Henry VII over the Cornish
     insurgents on Blackheath in Kent in 1497. Lancashire, pp. 97–8, suggests that
     there is a reference to Henry's French wars of 1489–92. But the geographical
     location of the places is perhaps not important; the usual function of the names
     in these bragging speeches is to produce an effect of bathos, by the inclusion of
     familiar, local names alongside distant, exotic ones. Herod's domain, in the
     Towneley *Herod the Great* 46–7, extends

     From Paradise to Padwa to Mownte Flascon,
     From Egypt to Mantua unto Kemp towne.

     There is a similar speech, with a longer catalogue of names, in *Hick Scorner*
     308–24.
258 *Brigand harness* ed (Brygaunt Ernys Q) This is taken as a name by Schell and
     Shuchter, *English Morality Plays*, p. 176; but no such figure is known, and the
     emendation (meaning 'the armour of brigands') is consistent with early spelling
     and grammar, and seems to be echoed in line 260.
260 *beaten, as Stephen was with stones* Stephen, saint and protomartyr, was stoned to
     death by the Jews *c.* A.D. 35 (see Acts of the Apostles 6–7).

So fell a fighter in a field was there never i-found;
To me no man is maked,
For Manhood Mighty, that is my name.
Many a lord have I do lame—
Wonder wide walketh my fame— 265
And many a king's crown have I cracked.

I am worthy and wight, witty and wise;
I am royal arrayed to reaven under the rice,
I am proudly apparelled in purpur and bice;
As gold I glister in gear. 270
I am stiff, strong, stalworth, and stout;
I am the royallest, redely, that runneth in this rout;
There is no knight so grisly that I dread nor doubt,
For I am so doughtily dight there may no dint me dere.

And the king of Pride full prest with all his proud presence, 275
And the king of Lechery lovely his letters hath me sent,
And the king of Wrath full worthily with all his intent—
They will me maintain with main and all their might;
The king of Covetise, and the king of Gluttony,
The king of Sloth, and the king of Envy— 280
All those send me their livery.
Where is now so worthy a wight?

---

261 *fell* fierce
262 *maked* matched, equal
264 *do lame* made lame
265 *walketh* spreads, extends
267 *wight* strong
268 *reaven under the rice* rob under the branches
270 *glister in gear* gleam in my armour
272 *that runneth in this rout* that is amongst this crowd
273 *doubt* fear
274 *I am ... dere* I am so strongly armed that no blow can harm me
277 *worthily* ed (wordely Q)
277 *intent* effort, attention
282 *wight* man

---

269 *purpur and bice* fine cloth of purple and blue-grey, often associated with royalty and wealth. Cf. John Gower, *Confessio Amantis* 6.986–90: 'Ther was a riche man/... so delicat/Of his clothing, that everyday/Of pourpre and bisse he made him gay'.
276 *letters* i.e. letters patent, by which a king confers rights and privileges.

A wight—
Yea, as a wight witty,
Here in this seat sit I;   285
For no loves let I
Here for to sit.

[*Sits. Enter* CONSCIENCE]

CONSCIENCE
Christ, as he is crowned king,
Save all this comely company,
And grant you all his dear blessing,   290
That bonerly bought you on the rood-tree!

Now pray you prestly, on every side,
To God omnipotent,
To set our enemy sharply on side,
That is the devil and his covent;   295

And all men to have a clear knowing
Of heaven bliss, that high tower.
Methink it is a necessary thing
For young and old, both rich and poor,

Poor Conscience for to know—   300
For Conscience clear it is my name.
Conscience counselleth both high and low,
And Conscience commonly beareth great blame—
Blame,
Yea, and oftentimes set in shame!   305
Wherefore I rede you men, both in earnest and in game,
Conscience that ye know;

For I know all the mysteries of man—
They be as simple as they can.
And in every company where I come   310
Conscience is out-cast;
All the world doth Conscience hate.

286 *For no loves let I* For no consideration will I cease
291 *bought* redeemed
291 *rood-tree* cross
292 *prestly* earnestly
295 *covent* assembly
298 *necessary* ed (nessarye Q)
306 *rede* advise

Mankind and Conscience ben at debate.
For if mankind might Conscience take
My body would they brast—   315

Brast,
Yea, and work me much woe!

MANHOOD

Say, ho, fellow! Who gave thee leave this way to go?
What! Weenest thou I dare not come thee to?
Say, thou harlot, whither in haste?   [*Seizes him*]   320

CONSCIENCE

What! Let me go, sir! I know you nought!

MANHOOD

No, bitched brothel, thou shalt be taught!
For I am a knight, and I were sought;
The World hath advanced me.

CONSCIENCE

Why, good sir knight, what is your name?   325

MANHOOD

Manhood, mighty in mirth and in game.
All power of Pride have I tane.
I am as gentle as jay on tree.

CONSCIENCE

Sir, though the World have you to manhood brought,
To maintain manner ye were never taught;   330
No, Conscience clear ye know right nought,
And this longeth to a knight.

MANHOOD

Conscience? What the devil man is he?

CONSCIENCE

Sir, a teacher of the spirituality.

MANHOOD

Spirituality? What the devil may that be?   335

313 *ben at debate* are at odds
315 *brast* break
319 *Weenest* Think
320 *harlot* scoundrel
322 *bitched brothel* vile scoundrel
323 *and I were sought* if my credentials were examined
327 *tane* taken
330 *manner* moderation
332 *longeth* is appropriate

316 *Brast* The word is printed in Q as part of line 317, and is here made a separate
   line by analogy with line 283.

CONSCIENCE
  Sir, all that be leaders into light.

MANHOOD
  Light? Yea, but hark, fellow, yet! Light fain would I see.
CONSCIENCE
  Will ye so, sir knight? Then do after me.
MANHOOD
  Yea, and it to Pride's pleasing be,
  I will take thy teaching.   340
CONSCIENCE
  Nay, sir, beware of pride, and you do well.
  For pride Lucifer fell into hell—
  Till doomsday there shall he dwell,
  Withouten any outcoming—

  For pride, sir, is but a vain glory.   345
MANHOOD
  Peace, thou brothel, and let those words be!
  For the World and Pride hath advanced me;
  To me men lout full low.
CONSCIENCE
  And to beware of pride, sir, I would you counsel;
  And think on King Robert of Cisell,   350
  How he for pride in great poverty fell,
  For he would not Conscience know.

MANHOOD
  Yea, Conscience, go forth thy way,
  For I love Pride, and will go gay;

339 *and* if
339 *pleasing* pleasure
345 *vain* worthless
348 *lout* bow
349 *you counsel* ed (counsayll you Q)
354 *gay* finely dressed

---

342 *Lucifer* According to Saint Jerome, Lucifer is the principal fallen angel, who
    must ever lament the loss of his former glory, which was bright as the morning
    star (*Catholic Encyclopedia*). The legend is apocryphal, but is based on refer-
    ences in Isaiah 14:12 and Luke 10:18; it was extremely influential in medieval
    literature and art, and is the subject of the first play in the mystery cycles.
350 *Robert of Cisell* King Robert of Sicily, whose throne, according to an exemplary
    story which was the subject of a Middle English romance, was usurped by an
    angel until the proud and boastful king learned proper humility. See L. H.
    Hornstein, *PMLA* 79 (1964), 13–21.

All thy teaching is not worth a stray,   355
For Pride clepe I my king.
CONSCIENCE
Sir, there is no king but God alone,
That bodily bought us with pain and passion,
Because of man's soul redemption—
In scripture thus we find.   360

MANHOOD
Say, Conscience, sith thou wouldest have Pride fro me.
What sayest thou by the king of Lechery?
With all mankind he must be,
And with him I love to leng.
CONSCIENCE
Nay, Manhood, that may not be;   365
From lechery fast you flee.
For in cumbrance it will bring thee
And all that to him will lend.

MANHOOD
Say, Conscience, of the king of Sloth;
He hath behight me mickle troth;   370
And I may not forsake him for ruth,
For with him I think to rest.
CONSCIENCE
Manhood, in scripture thus we find
That Sloth is a traitor to Heaven King;
Sir knight, if you will keep your king,   375
From sloth clean you cast.

355 *stray* straw
358 *bodily bought us* redeemed us with his body
358 *passion* suffering
359 *Because ... redemption* For the sake of the redemption of man's soul
361 *sith* since
361 *fro* from
364 *leng* abide
367 *cumbrance* trouble
368 *lend* come
370 *behight me mickle troth* sworn great promises to me
371 *ruth* pity
376 *From ... cast* Keep yourself well away from sloth

MANHOOD

Say, Conscience, the king of Gluttony—
He sayeth he will not forsake me,
And I purpose his servant to be,
With main and all my might.   380

CONSCIENCE

Think, Manhood, on substance,
And put out gluttony for cumbrance,
And keep with you good governance,
For this longeth to a knight.

MANHOOD

What, Conscience? From all my masters thou wouldest
    have me!   385
But I will never forsake Envy,
For he is king of company,
Both with more and less.

CONSCIENCE

Nay, Manhood, that may not be;
And ye will cherish envy,   390
God will not well pleased be
To comfort you in that case.

MANHOOD

Ey, ey! From five kings thou hast counselled me;
But from the king of Wrath I will never flee,
For he is in every deed doughty;   395
For him dare no man rout.

CONSCIENCE

Nay, Manhood, beware of wrath,
For it is but superfluity that cometh and goeth;
Yea, and all men his company hateth,
For oft they stand in doubt.   400

382 *for cumbrance* to avoid trouble
388 *less* ed (lasse r.w. case Q)
388 *Both with more and less* With people of all ranks
390 *And* If
396 *For ... rout* In his presence no one dares behave riotously

---

381 *substance* is the permanent quality which underlies outward appearances (*acci-dent*). Chaucer's Pardoner (*Canterbury Tales* C 538–40) speaks of cooks who 'stampe, and streyne, and grynde,/And turnen substaunce into accident'.

MANHOOD

Fie on thee, false flattering friar!
Thou shalt rue the time that thou came here.
The devil mote set thee on a fire
That ever I with thee met!
For thou counsellest me from all gladness,   405
And would me set unto all sadness;
But, ere thou bring me in this madness,
The devil break thy neck!

But, sir friar—evil mote thou thee—
From six kings thou hast counselled me,   410
But that day shall thou never see
To counsel me from Covetise.

CONSCIENCE

No, sir, I will not you from Covetise bring,
For Covetise I clepe a king.
Sir, Covetise in good doing   415
Is good in all wise.

But, sir knight, will ye do after me,
And Covetise your king shall be?

MANHOOD

Ye, sir, my troth I plight to thee
That I will work at thy will.   420

CONSCIENCE

Manhood, will ye by this word stand?

MANHOOD

Yea, Conscience, here my hand.
I will never from it fang,
Neither loud ne still.

401 *friar* ed (frere r.w. here Q)
403 *The devil mote* May the devil
409 *evil mote thou thee* ill may you thrive, i.e. curse you
417 *do after me* follow my advice
423 *fang* swerve
424 *loud ne still* loud nor quiet, i.e. under any circumstances

401 *friar* The reputation of the friars was so bad that the name of their order became
a common term of abuse. In this play, however, Conscience probably *is* a friar,
'a teacher of the spirituality' (line 334). Craik, p. 55, points out that the virtues
in the early Morality Plays usually wore clerical dress. On the friars generally
see J. J. Jusserand, *English Wayfaring Life* (London, 1961), pp. 159–74, and cf.
Mankind 325–6 and note.

CONSCIENCE

Manhood, ye must love God above all thing;   425
His name in idleness ye may not ming;
Keep your holy day from worldly doing;
Your father and mother worship aye;
Covet ye to slay no man;
Ne do no lechery with no woman;   430
Your neighbour's good take not by no way,
And all false witness ye must denay;

Neither ye must not covet no man's wife,
Nor no good that him belieth.
This covetise shall keep you out of strife.   435
These ben the commandments ten;
Mankind, and ye these commandments keep
Heaven bliss I you behete;
For Christ's commandments are full sweet,
And full necessary to all men.   440

MANHOOD

What, Conscience, is this thy Covetise?

CONSCIENCE

Yea, Manhood, in all wise.
And covet to Christ's service,
Both to matins and to mass.
Ye must, Manhood, with all your might   445
Maintain holy church's right,
For this longeth to a knight
Plainly in every place.

426 *ming* mention
427 *from worldly doing* free from worldly occupations
431 *good* goods, property
432 *denay* deny
434 *belieth* belongs to
438 *behete* promise
439 *are* ed (all Q)

425ff Conscience now instructs Manhood to follow the Ten Commandments of
    God, seeking to reverse Manhood's earlier commitment to the commandments
    of the World (cf. line 118).
443–4 *covet . . . mass* aspire to serve Christ both at matins and at mass. Matins was
    the public service preceding the first mass on Sunday, and in monastic life was
    one of the canonical hours. Cf. *Mankind* 711n.
445–7 A knight's first oath at creation was to love God and sustain the church (see
    lines 199–203n).

MANHOOD
  What, Conscience? Should I leave all game and glee?
CONSCIENCE
  Nay, Manhood, so mote I thee;   450
  All mirth in measure is good for thee;
  But, sir, measure is in all thing.
MANHOOD
  Measure, Conscience? What thing may measure be?
CONSCIENCE
  Sir, keep you in charity,
  And from all evil company,   455
  For doubt of folly doing.

MANHOOD
  Folly? What thing callest thou folly?
CONSCIENCE
  Sir, it is pride, wrath, and envy,
  Sloth, covetise, and gluttony;
  Lechery the seventh is—   460
  These seven sins I call folly.
MANHOOD
  What? Thou liest! To this seven the World delivered me,
  And said they were kings of great beauty,
  And most of main and mights.

  But yet I pray thee, sir, tell me.   465
  May I not go arrayed honestly?
CONSCIENCE
  Yes, Manhood, hardily,
  In all manner of degree.
MANHOOD
  But I must have sporting of play?
CONSCIENCE
  Sickerly, Manhood, I say not nay;   470

450 *so mote I thee* as I hope to prosper (an asseveration)
456 *For doubt of* For fear of
462 *What . . . me* ed (two lines in Q)
464 *mights* ed (myghtes r.w. seuente is Q)
466 *arrayed honestly* decently, becomingly dressed
467 *hardily* certainly
469 *have sporting of play* enjoy myself
470 *Sickerly* certainly

---

452 *measure is in all thing* proverbial (cf. Oxford Proverbs, p. 520; Tilley, M 806;
    Whiting, M 464, 'There is measure in all things'). Compare also the proverb
    'Measure is treasure' (*Mankind* 237 and note).

But good governance keep both night and day,
And maintain meekness and all mercy.

MANHOOD
All mercy, Conscience? What may that be?
CONSCIENCE
Sir, all discretion that God gave thee.
MANHOOD
Discretion I know not, so mote I thee!   475
CONSCIENCE
Sir, it is all the wits that God hath you send.

MANHOOD
Ah, Conscience, Conscience! Now I know and see
Thy cunning is much more than mine.
But yet I pray thee, sir, tell me,
What is most necessary for man in every time?   480

CONSCIENCE
Sir, in every time beware of folly;
Folly is full of false flattering;
In what occupation that ever ye be,
Alway, ere ye begin, think on the ending,
For blame.   485
Now farewell, Manhood; I must wend.
MANHOOD
Now farewell, Conscience, mine own friend.
CONSCIENCE
I pray you, Manhood, have God in mind,
And beware of Folly and Shame.

MANHOOD
Yes, yes, yea, come wind and rain,   490
God let him never come here again!

---

475 *so mote I thee* as I hope to prosper (an asseveration)
476 *wits* senses, intelligence (probably both meanings)
478 *cunning* knowledge

475–6 *Discretion ... send* Discretion and Five Wits are separate characters in
     Everyman.
484 *ere ye begin, think on the ending* proverbial (cf. *Oxford Proverbs*, p. 220; Tilley,
     E 128; Whiting, E 84). Compare also *Everyman* 10–11, 'in the beginning/Look
     well, and take good heed to the ending'.
490 *come wind and rain* a traditional saying (cf. Whiting, W 300, who cites 'Come
     wynde come reyne, come he never a-gayne'). A similar expression is in *Man-
     kind* 154.

Now he is forward, I am right fain,
For in faith, sir, he had near counselled me all amiss.

[*Exit* CONSCIENCE]

Ah, ah, now I have bethought me! If I shall heaven win,   495
Conscience teaching I must begin,
And clean forsake the kings of sin
That the World me taught;
And Conscience servant will I be,
And believe, as he hath taught me,
Upon one God and persons three,   500
That made all thing of nought;

For Conscience clear I clepe my king,
And am his knight in good doing;
For right of reason, as I find,   505
Conscience teaching true is.
The World is full of boast,
And saith he is of might's most;
All his teaching is not worth a cost,
For Conscience he doth refuse.

But yet will I him not forsake,   510
For mankind he doth merry make;
Though the World and Conscience be at debate,
Yet the World will I not despise,
For both in church and in cheaping,
And in other places being,   515
The World findeth me all thing,
And doth me great service.

492 *forward* gone
494 *bethought me* realized
495 *Conscience* Conscience's
500 *persons three* the Trinity, three persons in one God
503 *am* ed (om Q)
505 *true is* ed (is trewe Q)
514 *cheaping* market-place

494ff The apparent inconsistencies in Manhood's soliloquy are best explained as
     signs of his turmoil of mind.
502 *Conscience clear I clepe my king* This reverses 'Pride clepe I my king' of line 356.
508 *cost* something of little or no value, possibly an apocopated form of *costard*,
     'apple', or a mistake for *tost* (cf. the N-Town *death of Herod* 133: 'Ther is no lord
     like on live to me wurth a toost', where the expression seems to mean 'not worth
     a turd').

Now here full prest
I think to rest;
Now mirth is best.   520

[*Enter* FOLLY]

FOLLY

What, heigh-ho! Care away!
My name is Folly; I am not gay.
Is here any man that will say nay,
That runneth in this rout?
Ah, sir, God give you good eve!   525

MANHOOD

Stand utter, fellow! Where dost thou thy courtesy preve?

FOLLY

What? I do but claw mine arse, sir, by your leave.
I pray you, sir, rive me this clout.

518 *full prest* immediately
519 *to rest* ed (to ro rest Q)
526 *utter* further away
526 *preve* learn
527 *claw* scratch

522ff The appearance and demeanour of Folly are problematic. Is he melancholy or
       merry? Is he finely dressed or in the tatters of a tinker? Manly emends line 522
       to 'Am I not gay', making Folly the typical braggart, boasting of his fine
       appearance and threatening those who disagree (523–4). In that case the
       heigh-ho of line 522 would signal gaiety, as in medieval song refrains (see *MED*
       under *hei*). But if line 522 is allowed to stand as in Q, the *heigh-ho* must signify
       'an exclamation ... expressing yawning, sighing, languor, weariness, dis-
       appointment' (*OED*, though citing no instance earlier than 1553). This
       accords with Folly's claim to be out of luck (532–6), and with the implication
       that he is dressed in the poor clothes of a craftsman (528, 538). In view of the
       uncertainty, line 522 is here kept as in Q. But see also 537–8n.
528 *rive me this clout* appears to mean literally 'tear this piece of cloth for me',
     perhaps referring to Folly's attire. But in view of the context and Manhood's
     reaction there is probably some other meaning, such as 'scratch my arse for me'.
     Schell and Shuchter, *English Morality Plays*, p. 184, conjecture 'tear out this
     lump'.

MANHOOD

What! Stand out, thou sained shrew!

FOLLY

By my faith, sir, there the cock crew;   530
For—I take record of this row—
My theedom is near past.

MANHOOD

Now, truly, it may well be so.

FOLLY

By God, sir, yet have I fellows mo,
For in every country where I go   535
Some man his thrift hath lost.

MANHOOD

But hark, fellow, art thou any craftsman?

---

530 *By my* ed (By by Q)
531 *I ... row* I call this row of people (the audience) to witness
531 *row* ed (rewe r.w. shrewe, crewe Q)
532 *theedom* prosperity
534 *mo* more, as well
536 *thrift* prosperity, luck

---

529 *sained* A puzzling word which, if it is not a corruption of some other, seems to
be from *sain*, 'To make the sign of the cross on (a thing or person) in token of
consecration or blessing; or for the purpose of exorcizing a demon, warding off
the evil influences of witches, poison, etc.' (*OED*). *Sained* therefore could
mean 'blessed' (cf. present-day 'blessed' in its pejorative sense), or refer to the
thing exorcized, hence 'cursed'.

530 *there the cock crew* The various proverbs to which this remark seems to be
related offer no clear explanation. Whiting, C 347, cites Peter Idley (*c.* 1450):
'Ever the yonge cok croweth as the olde precheth' and Heywood (1546): 'The
yonge cocke croweth, as he the olde heereth'. Perhaps the meaning is 'there you
were speaking the truth [that I am cursed]'. Skelton's poetry contains instances
of 'In fayth, dicken, thou krew', which Dyce suggests may be 'the commence-
ment of some song' (see A. Dyce (ed), *John Skelton: the Poetical Works*
(London, 1843) I, 44, 170; II, 28, 115).

537–8 *craftsman ... tink a pan* Folly is perhaps dressed as a tinker, or perhaps carries
a pan, like Beelzebub in the Mummers' Plays. It is just possible that Folly is not
so dressed, but that *bind a sieve* and *tink a pan* are slang terms relating to
sword-play. In that case, *craftsman* might imply *craft of arms*, 'military knowledge, skill in warfare' (*MED*). Lancashire, pp. 98–100, argues that Folly may
have been meant to suggest William Empson and Edmund Dudley, two hated
administrators of Henry VII, and points out that Empson was mocked for his
low birth, and his father (incorrectly) made out to be a sievemaker.

FOLLY

    Yea, sir, I can bind a sieve and tink a pan,
    And thereto a curious buckler-player I am.
    Arise, fellow; will thou assay?   540

MANHOOD

    Now truly, sir, I trow thou canst but little skill of play.

FOLLY

    Yes, by Cock's bones, that I can.
    I will never flee for no man
    That walketh by the way.

MANHOOD

    Fellow, though thou have cunning,   545
    I counsel thee leave thy boasting,
    For here thou may thy fellow find,
    Whither thou wilt, at long or short.

FOLLY

    Come, look, and thou darest! Arise and assay!

MANHOOD

    Yea, sir, but yet Conscience biddeth me nay.   550

FOLLY

    No, sir, thou darest not, in good fay!
    For truly thou failest no false heart!

MANHOOD

    What sayest thou? Have I a false heart?

FOLLY

    Yea, sir, in good fay!

---

538 *tink* mend
539 *And ... am* And I am also a skilful sword-and-buckler player
541 *thou ... play* you know very little about sport, sword-play
542 *Cock's* God's (a common distortion)
551 *fay* faith
552 *thou failest no false heart* you are not without a cowardly heart

---

548 *long or short* Cf. George Silver, *Paradoxes of Defence* (London, 1599): 'Wherein
    is proved the true grounds of Fight to be in the short auncient weapons, and
    that the short Sword hath aduantage of the long Sword or Rapier'. At the time
    of *Mundus et Infans* the fashion of rapier-play was just being introduced into
    England from continental Europe. Manhood therefore claims superiority in
    the use of both new-style and traditional weapons.

MANHOOD

    Manhood will not that I say nay.   555
    Defend thee, Folly, if thou may!
    For, in faith, I purpose to wit what thou art.
                [They fence. FOLLY *is hit]*

    How sayest thou now, Folly, hast thou not a touch?

FOLLY

    No, iwis; but a little on my pouch—
    On all this meinie I will me vouch   560
    That standeth here about.

MANHOOD

    And I take record on all this row,
    Thou hast two touches, though I say but few.

FOLLY

    Yea, this place is not without a shrew!
    I do you all out of due.   565

MANHOOD

    But hark, fellow, by thy faith; where was thou bore?

FOLLY

    By my faith, in England have I dwelled yore,
    And all mine ancestors me before;
    But, sir, in London is my chief dwelling.

MANHOOD

    In London? Where, if a man thee sought?   570

---

559 *but a little* just a little one
560 *meinie* crowd (the audience)
562 *row* ed (rewe r.w. fewe, shrewe Q)
563 *though I say but few* even if I don't mention them all
565 *I do you all out of due* I absolve you all of your duty (the task of adjudicating the swordfight)
566 *bore* born
567 *yore* for a long time
570 *if a man thee sought* if one were to come looking for you

---

556 *if thou* ed (yftyou Q). The reading in Q obscures the force of the personal pronouns. Both Folly and Manhood use the impolite *thou* here, but when Folly wishes to ingratiate himself (e.g. at line 647) he uses *ye*. See A. C. Baugh, *A History of the English Language* (London, 1959), pp. 292–3.
558 *touch* hit. Even today, the acknowledgement of a hit at fencing is 'Touché!'
564 *this place is not without a shrew* Folly is annoyed that the audience has not supported him. Similar licence with regard to the audience is shown in *Jack Juggler*, p. 32, 'Many here smell strong'; for this and other instances see Craik, pp. 22–4.

FOLLY

Sir, in Holborn I was forth brought,
And with the courtiers I am betaught.
To Westminster I used to wend.

MANHOOD

Hark, fellow; why dost thou to Westminster draw?

FOLLY

For I am a servant of the law.   575
Covetise is mine own fellow;
We twain plead for the king;
And poor men that come from upland,
We will take their matter in hand;
Be it right or be it wrong,   580
Their thrift with us shall wend.

MANHOOD

Now hear, fellow, I pray thee; whither wendest thou then?

FOLLY

By my faith, sir, into London I ran,
To the taverns to drink the wine;
And then to the inns I took the way,   585
And there I was not welcome to the ostler,
But I was welcome to the fair tapster,
And to all the household I was right dear,
For I have dwelled with her many a day.

MANHOOD

Now I pray thee, whither took thou the way then?   590

---

577 *for* before
578 *upland* country areas
579 *matter* legal business, suits
582 *then* ed (than r.w. ran Q)
590 *the way then* ed (than the waye Q)

571–3 *Holborn ... Westminster* Holborn was a great lawyers' quarter, which, like
Westminster, was known at this time as a haunt of whores and thieves. See
Sugden, pp. 252–3, 560.
581 *Their ... wend* Their money (i.e. their legal costs) will go with us (i.e. into our
pockets). With the money Folly goes to taverns (584).
585 *the inns* This refers either to ordinary hostelries or to the Inns of Court, the
great legal centre in London. They constituted a sort of legal university and had
a reputation for rowdiness (Sugden, p. 268).
586 *not welcome to the ostler* Either Folly was not welcome because of the chance that
he might steal a horse, or (more probably) because, being no gentleman, he had
no horse for the ostler to tend.

FOLLY

In faith, sir, over London Bridge I ran,
And the straight way to the stews I came,
And took lodging for a night;
And there I found my brother, Lechery.
There men and women did folly,   595
And every man made of me as worthy
As though I had been a knight.

MANHOOD

I pray thee, yet tell me mo of thine adventures.

FOLLY

In faith, even straight to all the friars,
And with them I dwelled many years,   600
And they crowned Folly a king.

MANHOOD

I pray thee, fellow, whither wendest thou tho?

FOLLY

Sir, all England to and fro,
Into abbeys and into nunneries also;
And alway Folly doth fellows find.   605

MANHOOD

Now hark, fellow; I pray thee tell me thy name.

FOLLY

Iwis, I hight both Folly and Shame.

MANHOOD

Aha! Thou art he that Conscience did blame,
When he me taught.
I pray thee, Folly, go hence, and follow not me. 610

FOLLY

Yes, good sir, let me your servant be.

MANHOOD

Nay, so mote I thee!
For then a shrew had I caught.

FOLLY

Why, good sir, what is your name?

MANHOOD

Manhood mighty, that beareth no blame.   615

592 *stews* brothels
599 *friars* ed (freres r.w. aduentures, yeres Q)
605 *fellows* like-minded companions

FOLLY
> By the rood, and Manhood mistereth in every game
> Somedeal to cherish Folly,
> For Folly is fellow with the World,
> And greatly beloved with many a lord;
> And if ye put me out of your ward, 620
> The World right wrath will be.

MANHOOD
> Yea, sir, yet had I liefer the World be wrath,
> Than lose the cunning that Conscience me gave.

FOLLY
> A cuckoo for Conscience! He is but a daw;
> He cannot else but preach. 625

MANHOOD
> Yea, I pray thee leave thy lewd clattering,
> For Conscience is a counsellor for a king.

FOLLY
> I would not give a straw for his teaching.
> He doth but make men wrath.

> But wottest thou what I say, man? 630
> By that ilk truth that God me gave,
> Had I that bitched Conscience in this place,
> I should so beat him with my staff
> That all his stones should stink.

MANHOOD
> I pray thee, Folly, go hence and follow not me. 635

616 *rood* cross
616 *mistereth* needs
620 *ward* protection
622 *liefer* rather
624 *daw* fool
626 *lewd* ignorant
631 *ilk* same
634 *stones* testicles

---

627 *counsellor for a king* Cf. John Gower, *Confessio Amantis* 8. 2109–10: 'conseil
passeth alle thing/To him which thenkth to ben a king'.
633–4 *beat...stink* Cf. *Jack Juggler*, p. 20: 'beat on me, till I stink'; and p. 29: 'beat
me, till I fart and shit again'.

FOLLY
　　Yes, sir, so mote I thee,
　　Your servant will I be;
　　I axe but meat and drink.

MANHOOD
　　Peace, man! I may not have thee for thy name,
　　For thou sayest thy name is both Folly and Shame.   640
FOLLY
　　Sir, here in this clout I knit Shame,
　　And clepe me but proper Folly.   [*Removes his cloak*]
MANHOOD
　　Yea, Folly, will thou be my true servant?
FOLLY
　　Yea, Sir Manhood, here my hand.
MANHOOD
　　Now let us drink at this comnant,   645
　　For that is courtesy.

FOLLY
　　Marry, master, ye shall have in haste.
　　[*Aside*] Aha, sirs, let the cat wink!
　　For all ye wot not what I think.
　　I shall draw him such a draught of drink   650
　　That Conscience he shall away cast.
　　　　　　　　　　　　　　[*Gives him a drink*]

638 *axe but meat* ask only food
639 *for thy name* because of your reputation
645 *comnant* covenant, agreement

641–2 *here ... Folly* I wrap up Shame here in this garment, and call myself just
　　plain Folly. This interpretation accords with the extremely common practice in
　　the Morality Plays and Interludes of using changes of costume to signal changes
　　in spiritual condition (see Craik, pp. 73–92). The garment of Shame, cast off
　　by Folly at this point, becomes available for Manhood when he assumes the
　　name Shame at line 682.
648 *let the cat wink* said when a man closes his eyes to the consequences of his
　　actions. Whiting, C 96, and Tilley, C 152, cite Skelton (*c.* 1522): 'But swete
　　ypocras ye drynke,/With, Let the cat wynke!'
650–1 *I shall ... cast* both figuratively and literally true. Manhood will learn to sin
　　again by imbibing Folly's drink, and will become inebriated, from which will
　　arise both his false courage to reject Conscience and the means whereby Folly
　　dupes him.

Have, master, and drink well,
And let us make revel, revel!
For I swear by the church of Saint Michael,
I would we were at stews! 655
For there is nothing but revel-rout;
And we were there, I had no doubt
I should be knowen all about,
Where Conscience they would refuse.

MANHOOD
Peace, Folly, my fair friend, 660
For, by Christ, I would not that Conscience should me
here find.
FOLLY
Tush, master! Thereof speak nothing,
For Conscience cometh no time here.
MANHOOD
Peace, Folly! There is no man that knoweth me?
FOLLY
Sir, here my troth I plight to thee; 665
And thou wilt go thither with me,
For knowledge have thou no care.

MANHOOD
Peace! But it is hence a great way? .
FOLLY
Pardie, sir, we may be there on a day.
Yea, and we shall be right welcome, I dare well say, 670
In Eastcheap for to dine:
And then we will with Lombards at passage play,
And at The Pope's Head sweet wine assay.
We shall be lodged well a-fine.

656 *revel-rout* riotous merrymaking
667 *knowledge* being recognized
669 *Pardie* By God
672 *passage* dice
674 *a-fine* also, in short

671–3 *Eastcheap ... Pope's Head* Eastcheap was known for its taverns (especially
the Boar's Head which features in Shakespeare's *1 Henry IV*). Lombard Street,
off which ran Pope's Head Alley, where the tavern of that name stood, was
named after the Lombard money-changers, bankers, agents for foreign
traders, and money-lenders who carried out their business in that vicinity
(Sugden, pp. 165, 312, 418).

MANHOOD

What sayest thou, Folly; is this the best? 675

FOLLY

Sir, all this is manhood, well thou knowest.

MANHOOD

Now, Folly, go we hence in haste.
But fain would I change my name;
For, well I wot, if Conscience meet me in this tide,
Right well I wot, he would me chide. 680

FOLLY

Sir, for fear of you his face he shall hide.
I shall clepe you Shame.

MANHOOD

Now gramercy, Folly, my fellow in fere!
Go we hence—tarry no longer here—
Till we be gone, methink it, seven year. 685
I have gold and good to spend.

FOLLY

Aha, master, that is good cheer!
[*Aside*] And ere it be passed half a year,
I shall thee shear right a lewd friar,
And hither again thee send. 690

MANHOOD

Folly, go before, and teach me the way.

FOLLY

Come after, Shame, I thee pray,
And Conscience clear ye cast away.
[*To the audience*] Lo, sirs, this Folly teacheth aye;
For where Conscience cometh with his cunning, 695
Yet Folly full featly shall make him blind.
Folly before, and Shame behind—
Lo, sirs, thus fareth the world alway! [*Exit* FOLLY]

683 *in fere* in company (a rhyme tag)
685 *methink it* it seems to me, I should say
696 *featly shall make him blind* deftly, cleverly shall deceive him

689 *I shall ... friar* I shall shear (i.e. fleece) you as close as an ignorant, tonsured
friar. Cf. Chaucer's *Complaint to his Purse* 19: 'I am shave as nye as any frere'.

MANHOOD

    Now I will follow Folly, for Folly is my man;
    Yea, Folly is my fellow, and hath given me a name.   700
    Conscience called me Manhood: Folly calleth me Shame.

    Folly will me lead to London to learn revel:
    Yea, and Conscience is but a flattering brothel,
    For ever he is carping of care.
    The World and Folly counselleth me to all gladness: 705
    Yea, and Conscience counselleth me to all sadness;
    Yea, too much sadness might bring me into madness!
    And now have good day, sirs. To London to seek Folly will
        I fare.

        [*Enter* CONSCIENCE]

CONSCIENCE

    Say, Manhood, friend, whither will ye go?
MANHOOD

    Nay, sir, in faith my name is not so.   710
    Why, friar, what the devil hast thou to do
    Whether I go or abide?
CONSCIENCE

    Yes, sir, I will counsel you for the best.
MANHOOD

    I will none of thy counsel, so have I rest;
    I will go whither me list,   715
    For thou canst nought else but chide. [*Exit* MANHOOD]

CONSCIENCE

    Lo, sirs, a great ensample you may see—
    The frailness of mankind,
    How oft he falleth in folly
    Through temptation of the fiend;   720

704 *carping of care* prating about sorrow
706 *sadness* ed (sadnts Q)
711 *what ... do* what the devil has it to do with you
714 *so have I rest* as I hope to have rest (an asseveration)
715 *me list* ed (my lest r.w. best, rest Q)

699–701 Manly prints these lines as a six-line song; but a three-line stanza rhyming
    aaa occurs also at line 518, so they are best left as in Q.
709 *Say, Manhood* Manhood's change of name and garment cannot deceive Consci-
    ence. Cf. the rejection of Mercy under similar circumstances in *Mankind*
    725–8.

For when the fiend and the flesh be at one assent,
Then Conscience clear is clean out-cast.
Men think not on the great judgment
That the seely soul shall have at the last;

But would God all men would have in mind   725
Of the great day of doom,
How he shall give a great reckoning
Of evil deeds that he hath done.

But natheless, sith it is so
That Manhood is forth with Folly wend,   730
To seek Perseverance now will I go,
With the grace of God omnipotent;

His counsels ben in fere.
Perseverance counsel is most dear;
Next to him is Conscience clear   735
From sinning.
Now, into this presence, to Christ I pray,
To speed me well in my journey.
Farewell, lordings, and have good day!
To seek Perseverance will I wend.   740

[*Exit* CONSCIENCE *and enter* PERSEVERANCE]

PERSEVERANCE
Now, Christ, our comely creator, clearer than crystal
    clean,

---

724 *seely* poor
729 *natheless* ed (nedeles Q) nevertheless
733 *His ... fere* They are in each other's confidence
735–6 *clear/From sinning* furthest from sin
738 *journey* ed (Iournaye r.w. praye, daye Q)

---

727 *a great reckoning* The need to present an account of one's deeds at the Last
    Judgment is the main theme of *Everyman*; cf. also *Mankind* 861 and note.
731 *Perseverance* is also a character in *Hick Scorner* and *Magnificence*. What the
    name means is explained in *Perseverance*, partly by the alternative names for
    the castle, 'The Castle of Goodness' and 'The Castle of Virtue', but more
    explicitly by the text from Matthew 10:22 (identical with 24:13) which is there
    quoted after line 1705: 'He that shall persevere unto the end, he shall be saved'.
    Perseverance, therefore, is the *remedia*, or 'antidote', of Wanhope (cf. line 850
    and note). In pronunciation the main stress fell on the second syllable of the
    name.
741ff The status and virtue of Perseverance are conveyed through his elevated
    diction, which resembles that of Mercy in *Mankind*.

That craftily made every creature by good recreation,
Save all this company that is gathered here bedene,
And set all your souls into good salvation!

Now, good God, that is most wisest and wielder of wits, 745
This company counsel, comfort, and glad,
And save all this simplitude that seemly here sits!
Now, good God, for his mercy, that all men made—

Now, Mary, mother, meekest that I mean,
Shield all this company from evil inversation, 750
And save you from our enemy, as she is bright and clean,
And at the last day of doom deliver you from everlasting
    damnation.

Sirs, Perseverance is my name,
Conscience born brother that is;
He sent me hither mankind to indoctrine, 755
That they should to no vices incline;
For oft mankind is governed amiss,
And through Folly mankind is set in shame.
Therefore in this presence to Christ I pray,
Ere that I hence wend away, 760
Some good word that I may say
To borrow man's soul from blame.

[*Enter* AGE, *who does not see* PERSEVERANCE]

742 *craftily* skilfully
742 *recreation* creation anew
743 *bedene* together
745 *wielder of wits* ed (welde of wyttes Q) governor, controller of minds and senses
746 *glad* gladden
749 *mean* have in mind
750 *inversation* reversal, turning aside from the true course
751 *she* i.e. Mary
751 *clean* pure
754 *that* ed (om Q)
755 *indoctrine* teach
762 *borrow* protect, save

747 *this simplitude* ed (this symylytude Q) these good people (see *OED* under
simple). Lancashire, p. 97, suggests retaining the reading in Q with the meaning 'identical group', that is, a section of the audience sitting apart from those
who are referred to as 'This company' (746).

AGE

Alas, alas, that me is woe!
My life, my liking I have forlorn;
My rents, my richesse—it is all i-go;   765
Alas the day that I was born!

For I was born Manhood most of might,
Stiff, strong, both stalworthy and stout;
The World full worthily hath made me a knight;
All bowed to my bidding bonerly about.   770

Then Conscience clear, comely and kind,
Meekly he met me in seat there I sat;
He learned me a lesson of his teaching,
And the seven deadly sins full loathly he did hate:

Pride, wrath, and envy, and gluttony in kind—   775
The World all these sins delivered me until—
Sloth, covetise, and lechery, that is full of false flattering;
All these Conscience reproved both loud and still.

To Conscience I held up my hand,
To keep Christ's commandments.   780
He warned me of Folly, that traitor, and bade me beware,
And thus he went his way;
But I have falsely me forsworn.
Alas the day that I was born!
For body and soul I have forlorn.   785
I cling as a clod in clay.

In London many a day
At the passage I would play;
I thought to borrow and never pay.

---

764 *forlorn* completely lost
765 *i-go* gone
775 *gluttony* ed (couetous Q)
775 *in kind* carnal
776 *until* unto
778 *both loud and still* in every way
779 *held up my hand* raised my hand (in making an oath)
783 *me forsworn* gone back on my word

---

786 *I cling as a clod in clay* I shrivel up like a corpse in the earth. The completely
conventional character of this simile is symptomatic of this rather pedestrian
part of the play. The same image seems, in contrast, to spring to life in the
Towneley play of *Noah*, 62–3: 'As muk apon mold/I widder away'.

Then was I sought and set in stocks;   790
In Newgate I lay under locks;
If I said aught I caught many knocks.
Alas, where was Manhood tho?

Alas, my lewdness hath me lost.
Where is my body so proud and prest?   795
I cough and rout; my body will brest,
Age doth follow me so.
I stare and stacker as I stand,
I groan grisly upon the ground.
Alas, Death, why lettest thou me live so long?   800
I wander as a wight in woe

And care,
For I have done ill;
Now wend I will,
Myself to spill,   805
I care not whither nor where.

[PERSEVERANCE *comes forward*]

PERSEVERANCE
Well i-met, sir, well i-met; and whither away?
AGE
Why, good sir, whereby do ye say?

795 *prest* fit, active
796 *rout* belch
798 *stacker* stagger
798 *stand* ed (stonde r.w. grounde Q)
799 *grisly* ed (glysly Q) horribly
805 *spill* destroy, kill
807 *i-met* met
808 *whereby* why

---

791 *Newgate* one of the gates of old London, used as the city's chief prison until it
   was demolished in 1777 (Sugden, pp. 363–4).
795 *Where is ... prest* The words and the sentiment derive from the *ubi sunt* laments,
   moral poems consisting of long catalogues of rhetorical questions beginning *ubi
   sunt ... ?* ('where are ... ?') relating to the transience of wealth, health, beauty,
   and other worldly things. For examples see R. T. Davies, *Medieval English
   Lyrics* (London, 1963), Nos. 8, 83, 131.
800 *Death ... long* This is a subject of a number of medieval poems. Cf. Davies,
   Medieval Lyrics, Nos. 88, 149.
805 *Myself to spill* to kill myself. Suicide was the ultimate expression of the sin of
   wanhope, on which see line 850 and note, and cf. the near-suicide in *Mankind*
   799–806.

PERSEVERANCE
  Tell me, sir, I you pray,
  And I with you will wend.   810
AGE
  Why, good sir, what is your name?
PERSEVERANCE
  Forsooth, sir, Perseverance, the same.
AGE
  Sir, ye are Conscience brother, that me did blame!
  I may not with you leng.

PERSERVERANCE
  Yes, yes, Manhood, my friend in fere.   815
AGE
  Nay, sir, my name is in another manner;
  For Folly his own self was here
  And hath cleped me Shame.
PERSEVERANCE
  Shame? Nay, Manhood, let him go—
  Folly and his fellows also;   820
  For they would thee bring into care and woe,
  And all that will follow his game.

AGE
  Yea, game whoso game!
  Folly hath given me a name,
  So, wherever I go,   825
  He cleped me Shame.
  Now Manhood is gone,
  Folly hath followed me so.

  When I first from my mother came,
  The World made me a man,   830
  And fast in riches I ran,
  Till I was dubbed a knight;
  And then I met with Conscience clear,
  And he me set in such manner
  Methought his teaching was full dear,   835
  Both by day and night.

813 *Conscience ... blame* the brother of Conscience, who reprimanded me
814 *leng* remain
819 *Shame* ed (this word forms a separate line in Q)
823 *game whoso game* let whomsoever it pleases be merry

And then Folly met me,
And sharply he beset me,
And from Conscience he fet me;
He would not fro me go.   840
Many a day he kept me,
And to all folks Shame he cleped me,
And unto all sins he set me;
Alas, that me is woe!

For I have falsely me forsworn.   845
Alas, that I was born!
Body and soul, I am but lorn,
Me liketh neither glee nor game.

PERSEVERANCE
Nay, nay, Manhood, say not so!
Beware of Wanhope, for he is a foe.   850
A new name I shall give you to:
I clepe you Repentance;
For, and you here repent your sin,
Ye are possible heaven to win;
But with great contrition ye must begin,   855
And take you to abstinence;

For though a man had do alone
The deadly sins everychone,
And he with contrition make his moan
To Christ our heaven king,   860
God is also glad of him,
As of the creature that never did sin.

838 *beset* ensnared, attacked
839 *fet* fetched
842 *Shame he cleped me* ed (he cleped me/Fro shame Q)
847 *lorn* lost, ruined
848 *Me liketh* pleases me
854 *possible heaven to win* capable of reaching heaven
857 *do* done
858 *everychone* everyone
861 *also* as

---

850 *Wanhope* ed (wanhode Q) The fifteenth-century religious manual *Jacob's Well*,
   p. 113, describes wanhope as the sixth degree of sloth: 'Wanhope wyll makyn a
   man to holdyn [consider] hymself so synfull and cursed, that hym thynketh
   that he may noght ben amendyd . . . He wyll noght be schreuyn [confessed], ne
   repentyn hym, ne cryin god mercy. He thynketh that god were unryghtfull, yif
   he gaf hym mercy'.
857–62 Christ's explanation of the parable of the lost sheep (Luke 15:7). Cf.
   Mankind 770n.

AGE

Now, good sir, how should I contrition begin?

PERSEVERANCE

Sir, in shrift of mouth, without varying;

And another ensample I shall show you to: 865
Think on Peter and Paul, and other mo,
Thomas, James, and John also,
And also Mary Magdalene.
For Paul did Christ's people great villainy,
And Peter at the Passion forsook Christ thrice,   870
And Magdalene lived long in lechery,
And St Thomas believed not in the Resurrection;

And yet these to Christ are darlings dear,
And now be saints in heaven clear.
And therefore, though ye have trespassed here,   875
I hope ye be sorry for your sin.

AGE

Yea, Perseverance, I you plight,
I am sorry for my sin both day and night.
I would fain learn, with all my might,
How I should heaven win.   880

---

864 *varying* dispute
877 *plight* promise

863–4 *contrition . . . shrift of mouth* Age and Perseverance mention the first two of the
three parts of the sacrament of penance. The other is satisfaction. See *Everyman* 549n.

869 *Paul* The Acts of the Apostles 9:1–27 describes how Saul, a persecutor of
Christians, became converted and changed his name to Paul as the result of a
blinding vision outside Damascus.

870 *Peter* St Peter, in accordance with the prophecy of Jesus, denied Christ three
times before cockcrow after the arrest in the garden (Matthew 26:69–75, Mark
14:66–72; Luke 22:55–62).

871 *Magdalene* Mary Magdalene was regarded in the middle ages as the archetypal
fallen woman transformed into a saint. Her biography, the subject of many
stories and several plays (see, for example, Bevington, pp. 687–753), was
constructed from apocryphal legend and shadowy Biblical references, one of
the most important of which was to an unnamed sinful woman who washed the
feet of Christ with her tears (Luke 7:36–50).

872 *St Thomas* Thomas Didymus, a disciple of Jesus, refused to believe that Jesus
had risen until he had put his finger and hand into the wounds (John
20:24–29).

PERSEVERANCE
> Sir, to win heaven five necessary things there ben,
> That must be known to all mankind:
> The five wits doth begin,
> Sir, bodily and spiritually.

AGE
> Of the five wits I would have knowing. 885

PERSEVERANCE
> Forsooth, sir, hearing, seeing, and smelling,
> The remnant tasting and feeling—
> These ben the five wits bodily;
>
> And, sir, other five wits there ben.

AGE
> Sir Perseverance, I know not them. 890

PERSEVERANCE
> Now, Repentance, I shall you ken:
> They are the power of the soul:
> Clear in mind—there is one—
> Imagination, and all reason,
> Understanding, and compassion; 895
> These belong unto Perseverance.

AGE
> Gramercy, Perseverance, for your true teaching.
> But, good sir, is there any more behind
> That is necessary to all mankind
> Freely for to know? 900

881 *Sir* ed (So Q)
881 *necessary* ed (nessarye Q)
891 *ken* teach
898 *behind* in addition
900 *Freely* Fully

883 *five wits* The five bodily and spiritual senses are explained in the late
fourteenth-century *Lay Folk's Catechism*, pp. 18–19, though the 'inwits' (will,
reason, mind, imagination, and thought) are not the same as in the play. *Jacob's
Well*, pp. 222–3, is again different, listing will, understanding, mind, desire,
and delight. The church taught that both outward and inward senses needed to
be kept free from wickedness.

PERSEVERANCE
Yea, Repentance, more there be,
That every man must on believe:
The twelve articles of the faith,
That mankind must on trow.

The first, that God is in one substance,   905
And also that God is in three persons,
Beginning and ending without variance,
And all this world made of nought.
The second, that the Son of God sickerly
Took flesh and blood of the Virgin Mary,   910
Without touching of man's flesh-company—
This must be in every man's thought.

The third, that that same God Son,
Was born of that holy Virgin,
And she after his birth maiden as she was before,   915
And clearer in all kind.
Also the fourth, that same Christ, God and man,
He suffered pain and passion
Because of man's soul redemption,
And on a cross did hang.   920

The fifth article I shall you tell:
Then the spirit of Godhead went to hell,
And bought out the souls that there did dwell,
By the power of his own might.

904 *on trow* believe in
907 *variance* change
911 *flesh-company* sexual intercourse
914 *Was* ed (om Q)
915 *before* ed (beforne Q)
916 *clearer in all kind* purer in every respect

---

903 *The twelve articles of the faith* The classification of the basic tenets of the
Christian faith embodied in the Creed has varied with time. *The Lay Folks'
Catechism*, pp. 14–18, teaches twenty-three articles in three parts. Lydgate's
Pilgrimage of the Life of Man (ed F. J. Furnivall (London, EETS E.S.83, 1901),
6603–83) teaches twelve: belief in: 1. God the Father 2. Son 3. Holy Spirit 4.
Incarnation 5. Passion 6. Descent into Hell (to release the souls of the just from
Limbo) 7. Resurrection 8. Ascension 9. Holy Church 10. Communion of
Saints (the spiritual solidarity of saved souls) 11. Last Judgment 12. The final
rewards for the saved and punishments for the damned. The order is thus
different from that of the play, which also omits the seventh article (see line
929n).

The sixth article I shall you say: 925
Christ rose upon the third day,
Very God and man, withouten nay,
That all shall deem and dight.

He sent man's soul into heaven,
Aloft all the angels everychone,   930
There is the Father, the Son,
And the soothfast Holy Ghost.
The eighth article we must believe on:
That same God shall come down
And deem man's soul at the day of doom,   935
And on mercy then must we trust.

The ninth article, withouten strife:
Every man, maiden, and wife,
And all the bodies that ever bore life,
At the day of doom, body and soul, shall pear.   940
Truly the tenth article is:
All they that hath kept God's service
They shall be crowned in heaven bliss,
As Christ's servants to him full dear.

The eleventh article, the sooth to sayn: 945
All that hath falsely to God guided them,
They shall be put into hell pain—
There shall be no sin-covering.

927 *Very* True
927 *withouten nay* undeniably
928 *deem and dight* judge and dispose of, sentence
930 *Aloft* Above
931 *There* Where
931–2 *There ... Ghost* ed (one line in Q)
932 *soothfast* true
937 *withouten strife* unquestionably
940 *At* ed (And at Q)
940 *pear* appear
945 *sayn* say
946 *guided them* conducted themselves
948 *sin-covering* concealing of sin

929 *He sent man's soul into heaven* The list lacks any reference to the Ascension, and
since the seventh article is omitted, this line, which makes no sense in this
context, probably should read: 'He (Christ) ascended into heaven'.

Sir, after the twelfth we must work,
And believe in all the sacraments of holy church,   950
That they ben necessary to both last and first
To all manner of mankind.

Sir, ye must also hear and know the commandments ten.
Lo, sir, this is your belief and all men;
Do after it and ye shall heaven win—   955
Without doubt I know.

AGE

Gramercy, Perseverance, for your true teaching,
For in the spirit of my soul will I find
That it is necessary to all mankind
Truly for to know.   960

[*To the audience*]
Now, sirs, take all ensample by me,
How I was born in simple degree;
The World royal received me,
And dubbed me a knight;
Then Conscience met me;   965
So after him came Folly;
Folly falsely deceived me;
Then Shame my name hight.

PERSEVERANCE

Yea, and now is your name Repentance,
Through the grace of God almight.   970
And therefore, without any distance,
I take my leave of king and knight;
And I pray to Jesu, which has made us all,
Cover you with his mantle perpetual. Amen.

Here endeth the Interlude of Mundus et Infans, Imprinted at
London in Fleet Street at the Sign of the Sun by me, Wynkyn de
Worde, the year of our Lord MCCCCC and xxii, the xvii day of
July.

949 *work* ed (wyrche r.w. chyrche Q) strive
951 *to both last and first* i.e. to everyone
954 *men* men's
955 *Do after it* Act upon it
971 *without any distance* assuredly
973 *which* who
974 *mantle* i.e. protection

℧Here endeth the Interlude of Mundus & Infans.
Imprynted at London in Fleteſtrete at the ſygne of þ
Soñe by me Wynkyn de worde. The yere of our Lorde
M.CCCCC.and.xxij.The.xvij.daye of July.

Fig. 4. *Colophon of Mundus et Infans* [Q]